THE TRUTH BEHIND

LEFT

BEHIND

MARK HITCHCOCK
THOMAS ICE

Multnomah® Publishers *Sisters, Oregon*

THE TRUTH BEHIND LEFT BEHIND
published by Multnomah Publishers, Inc.

© 2004 by Mark Hitchcock and Thomas Ice
International Standard Book Number: 1-59052-366-0

Cover design by Brand Navigation, LLC
Cover art/photo by Iconica/Paul Edmondson

Unless otherwise indicated, Scripture quotations are from:
New American Standard Bible © 1960, 1977, 1995
by the Lockman Foundation. Used by permission.
Other Scripture quotations are from:
Holy Bible, New Living Translation (NLT)
© 1996. Used by permission of Tyndale House Publishers, Inc.
All rights reserved.
The Holy Bible, New International Version (NIV)
© 1973, 1984 by International Bible Society,
used by permission of Zondervan Publishing House

Multnomah is a trademark of Multnomah Publishers, Inc.,
and is registered in the U.S. Patent and Trademark Office.
The colophon is a trademark of Multnomah Publishers, Inc.

Printed in the United States of America

For information:
MULTNOMAH PUBLISHERS, INC. • P.O. BOX 1720 • SISTERS, OR 97759

Library of Congress Cataloging-in-Publication Data

Hitchcock, Mark.
  The truth behind Left behind / by Mark Hitchcock and Thomas Ice.
      p. cm.
Includes bibliographical references.
  ISBN 1-59052-366-0 (pbk.)
  1. Rapture (Christian eschatology) 2. Antichrist. 3. Beast of the Apocalypse.
4. Dispensationalism. 5. LaHaye, Tim F. Left behind series. I. Ice, Thomas. II.
Title.

BT887.H57 2004
236'.9—dc22

                                        2003026156

04 05 06 07 08 09 10—10 9 8 7 6 5 4 3 2 1 0

CONTENTS

INTRODUCTION

Tim LaHaye

W*hat's the secret behind the phenomenal popularity of the Left Behind fiction series that you and Jerry Jenkins wrote?"*

I'm asked that question wherever I go. Really, there are many reasons for the success of these books. The true account of the Rapture and the subsequent seven-year Tribulation period—as described so graphically in the book of Revelation—has to be the greatest story in the two thousand years since Christ ascended to His Father.

The natural interest in Bible prophecy—particularly in perilous days like ours—has many people turning to the Bible for answers about the future. Add to that the simple fact that Jerry B. Jenkins is a superb fiction writer with a phenomenal skill for taking my interpretation of end-time events and putting it into an exciting fictional setting.

Beyond all these things, however, I have to say simply that it's a "God thing."

The God who gave me the idea for a work of fiction based on the facts of future Bible prophecy and led me to partner with Jerry has chosen to bless the series beyond our wildest dreams. And the best part of all is that thousands of people have come to faith in Jesus Christ after reading the series.[1] Many thousands more have rededicated their lives to serve Him.

Sold in thirty-seven countries around the world, these books have helped countless believers and unbelievers alike to understand the wonderful plan God has for their future…and the future of all mankind. The letters that pour into our offices daily relate instance after instance of spiritual blessings resulting from the reading of these books.

That's what makes it so difficult to understand why several books have popped up trying to undercut and discredit the Left Behind series. I have personally communicated with several of the authors—Seventh-day Adventists, Catholic scholars, and particularly Reformed theologians who advocate the "preterist" concept that Christ came back in A.D. 70, at the destruction of Jerusalem. You would think they would be thrilled that multitudes of people worldwide are coming to Christ through these books. You would think they would be pleased that thousands more are being motivated to holy living, evangelism, and a renewed missionary vision. Why would any Christian object to these outcomes? But rather than celebrating this phenomenon, these critics seem upset and troubled that a literal interpretation of end-time prophecies is being popularized around the world.

I don't take their criticism personally.

It really isn't a matter of finding fault with Jerry and me, as much as it is criticizing the literal interpretation we bring to Bible prophecy. Even so, if these detractors had been paying attention during the last fifty years, as many modern translations of the Bible have become popular among laypeople, they would have realized the real secret to our books' popularity. The millions of new Bible readers who have come to Christ in the past five decades or so have found the Bible in their favorite translation to be engaging and exciting—a personal love letter from God their heavenly Father.

People are reading the Bible as never before. They are reading it and believing what they read. Just as it is written.

And why shouldn't they? After all, it comes from the hand of God Himself.

These readers take Scripture literally whenever possible—unless some false teacher has clouded their thinking, rendering prophecy virtually impossible to understand by trying to interpret it through symbols or confusing allegories.

When the millions of Christians (and even many unbelievers who respect the Bible) read one of our twelve books in the Left Behind series, they find the basic events portrayed just as they have read them in the pages of Scripture. That is why so many have said that these works of fiction drove them back to the Bible to check the facts. Almost invariably they find that our stories parallel the prophecies of the Scriptures. Jerry and I have unashamedly taken the position that all prophecy should be interpreted literally whenever possible. We have been guided throughout by the golden rule of interpretation: *When the plain sense of Scripture makes common sense, seek no other sense. Take every word at its primary, literal meaning unless the facts of the immediate context clearly indicate otherwise.*

One thing most of the detractors of our books have in common is a tendency to allegorize or spiritualize prophecy. Some take the rest of the Scripture literally, but insist that prophecy is somehow different. According to them, we need to be looking for some deeper, "secret" meaning other than the literal message conveyed by the words on the page. Once you begin heading down that road, however, everything is up for grabs. You can invent any kind of "interpretation" you want.

That's how some have come up with the bizarre idea that Jesus came back to this earth in A.D. 70—and that we've been living in the messianic kingdom age ever since.[2] According to the adherents of this view, Satan is already bound and we believers are on our way to converting the world before Christ returns.

Most believers find it easier to take Bible prophecies literally wherever possible, believing that Christ will indeed rapture His church to heaven, just as He promised in John 14:1–3. They believe that the earth will go through a seven-year Tribulation, as described in Revelation 6–18. And they believe that Christ will return in glory, set up His promised earthly kingdom for one thousand years (Revelation 19–20), and then take all believers to heaven to live with Him forever (Revelation 21–22). Obviously this literal interpretation is much easier to understand—and gives greater hope for humankind's future.

And we have plenty of precedent for taking prophecy literally. In our Lord's first coming, He literally fulfilled over 109 prophecies. Dr. John Walvoord, dean of twentieth-century prophecy scholars, identified one thousand prophecies in the Bible, *five hundred* of which have already been fulfilled...literally! Why should we expect anything less than a literal fulfillment of the five hundred future prophecies that remain?

In the opening words of Revelation, the Holy Spirit promises a special blessing to "he who reads and those who hear the words of the prophecy, and heed the things which are written in it" (1:3). But how do you get a blessing out of something you can't understand? The fact is, unless you take the book of Revelation literally, you will *never* understand it. The key to understanding and receiving blessing from this very exciting book is to take it literally, just as the Lord intended.

In addition to this matter of literal interpretation, there are perhaps a dozen other areas where the critics of Left Behind have taken their shots at our interpretation of end-time events. Rather than answering each detractor individually (none of us needs to get into a fruitless pattern of attack and counterattack), the writers of this book have wisely chosen to tackle the most common questions with solid biblical answers.

Multnomah Publishers could not have selected two more qualified prophecy scholars to answer these objections. Dr. Thomas Ice is a graduate of Dallas Theological Seminary, where he became one of the leading disciples of the late Dr. John Walvoord. He is currently executive director of the Pre-Trib Research Center and a highly respected prophecy scholar in his own right, with many books, articles, and monographs on these themes. Dr. Ice has debated many of the Reformed scholars and other preterists who attempt to allegorize prophecy. Mark Hitchcock is a popular writer of numerous books, a member of the Pre-Trib Study Group, and the editor of the on-line *Left Behind Newsletter,* found at www.leftbehind.com, all of this while pastoring a large and growing church, Faith Bible Church of Edmond, Oklahoma. Mark graduated from Dallas Theological Seminary and is only a dissertation away from receiving his PhD.

I commend Multnomah for publishing *The Truth Behind Left Behind.* Dr. Ice and Mark Hitchcock, both able writers as well as scholars, are qualified to answer our critics with sound, easy to understand explanations to the most common interpretations of Bible prophecy. Jerry Jenkins and I—as well as the authors of this valuable book—want the readers of the Left Behind series to look forward with great anticipation to the soon coming of Jesus and the Rapture of all believers before the great coming storm of His wrath. Once they capture the vision of the Savior's possible coming at any moment, they will have a greater passion to see that none of their loved ones or friends have to endure the terrible days of Tribulation that must come.

And that, my friends, is the compassionate truth behind Left Behind.

Tim LaHaye

PART ONE

HEADLINES

CHAPTER ONE

THE TRUTH BEHIND THE FICTION

The Left Behind series has enjoyed an incredible run in the publishing world.

Talk about understatement!

Left Behind has blown the lid off previous publishing records. It has been *wildly* successful. It's not just the new standard in the world of fiction; it's its own standard. And the juggernaut shows no signs of slowing down.

Millions of readers can't wait for the next installment. They mark the release date on their calendars and wait with eager anticipation—even prebuying the book weeks before it hits the shelves. They look forward to rejoining the story and continuing the breathtaking journey through the book of Revelation and the major events of the end times.

As you might well imagine, the success of the series has brought out two distinct and very different responses: one positive and one negative. This book was written to address both of these responses.

Beyond all doubt, the Left Behind series has led many people to assess or reassess their relationship to Jesus Christ. Authors Tim LaHaye and Jerry Jenkins have received thousands of accounts of people trusting Jesus Christ as their personal Savior from reading these books. At the same time, the series has also aroused a renewed interest in study of the end times—much as Hal Lindsay did with his milestone book *The Late Great Planet Earth* back in the early seventies. People who read the books are left wanting to know more about the climactic final days of our world as prophesied in the Bible.

Haven't you wondered, after reading these books, what the Bible really says about the final days of our world? Wouldn't you like to know more about the fact behind the fiction? Wouldn't it be great to know more about the Rapture, the Antichrist, the mark of the beast, and the future city of New Babylon?

If so, then this book is for you. One of our key reasons for writing this book was to provide the readers of the Left Behind books with more information on what the Bible says about God's plan for the ages. After all, everybody knows that Bible prophecy can sometimes (to put it modestly) be a bit confusing. Many sincere and diligent students of the Bible experience difficulty in attempting to sort it all out. This is where *The Truth Behind Left Behind* comes in. We wrote this book with you in mind, to help you gain a deeper understanding of the end times—and how some of the key persons, places, and events fit together.

But there is another reason for this book as well. Even though the Left Behind series has engaged millions of readers worldwide, a handful of well-placed critics have been calling into question the whole premise of these books. As we will see in the coming pages, these detractors are claiming that both the stories *and* the theology of the series are nothing but fiction.

We take strong issue with such attacks.

And we want to show you why.

THE DETRACTORS

We all know that when something—anything—enjoys great success, it will inevitably stir up some controversy. That's just the nature of things. Success always brings a swarm of critics. Detractors immediately begin lining up to take their best shot.

The Left Behind phenomenon is certainly no exception. People have criticized the series from every angle—even going so far as to question the intentions and motives of the authors and publisher.

If you think we're exaggerating, just go on-line and search for "Left Behind," "fiction," and other related words. You'll find dozens of articles and reviews attacking the fiction, faith, and alleged faulty end times theology of the series.[1]

But the most steady, sustained, serious criticism has come from those who say that the entire series is based on fiction. Of course, the series *is* fictional; what we have here are immensely entertaining stories. But what the critics mean is that the whole end time view of the series is nothing but fiction—that the future events portrayed in the story are completely fabricated and unbiblical.

In the last few years, numerous books, papers, and articles have tried to chip away at the very foundation of the series. They have leveled strong attacks on the entire theology or end time view that undergirds these books.

Among the detractors of Left Behind are some of the major Protestant denominations, such as the Presbyterian Church USA,[2] Seventh-day Adventists, and some fundamental Baptists.[3] Left Behind has also been strongly condemned by Roman Catholics as "anti-Catholic." Roman Catholics have stated clearly, "We don't believe in the rapture."[4]

Additionally, numerous books have been written with the express purpose of critiquing or in some cases even mocking the Left Behind view of the end times or some aspect of it.

Some of the better known books include:

- *End Times Fiction: A Biblical Consideration of the Left Behind Theology* (Gary DeMar, Nashville, TN: Thomas Nelson, 2001).

- *Will Catholics Be "Left Behind"? A Catholic Critique of the Rapture and Today's Prophecy Preachers* (Carl E. Olson, Ft. Collins, CO: Ignatius, 2003).
- *The Rapture Trap: A Catholic Response to "End Times" Fever* (Paul Thigpen, West Chester, PA: Ascension, 2001).
- *The Left Behind Deception: Revealing Dangerous Errors About the Rapture and the Antichrist* (Steve Wohlberg, Ft. Worth, TX: Texas Media Center, 2001).
- *IRAQ: Babylon of the End-Times?* (C. Marvin Pate and J. Daniel Hays, Grand Rapids, MI: Baker Book House, 2003).
- *I Want to Be Left Behind* (Ted Noel, Maitland, FL: BibleOnly Press, 2002).
- *I Want to Be "Left Behind": An Examination of the Ideas Behind the Popular Series and the End Times* (Tim Kirk, Campbell, CA: Writers Club Press, 2002).

Since the end time view of Left Behind is the foundation of the entire series, we believe these criticisms need to be addressed. Otherwise the credibility of these powerful volumes could be seriously undermined. After reading some of these critiques, people might be left wondering....

- *Have the authors totally misread and misunderstood Revelation?*
- *Is the Left Behind view of the end times unbiblical?*
- *Is there really going to be a rapture?*
- *Will millions truly be left behind?*
- *Does the Bible actually say that there will be a future, terrible time of tribulation?*

- *Will there be a future person called Antichrist who will rule the world?*
- *Will people really have to take the mark of the beast or die?*
- *Can people be saved after the Rapture?*

An undiscerning acceptance of the criticisms of Left Behind could easily lead unsuspecting readers to view the series just like any other *New York Times* fiction bestseller. It could take the cutting edge off the overriding message of the books—the need to receive Jesus Christ by faith as your Savior from sin before it's too late. It could even cause many who have believed the gospel from reading these books to entertain serious doubts. To wonder if it's all just fiction.

We don't want this to happen.

OUR PURPOSE

The purpose of this book is to take a fresh look at the end time view presented in the Left Behind series—and to demonstrate that it is firmly supported by both God's Word and church history. We want to make it clear at the outset that we harbor no ill feelings toward those who disagree with our view. We aren't writing this book because we dislike any person or group who has criticized Left Behind. Our purpose is not to condemn or make fun of the views of others, but rather to present what we believe is the biblical view of the end times in light of the mounting criticisms that have come against those teachings.

To accomplish this purpose, we want to take you step-by-step through the key events presented in the Left Behind series and show you what some of the critics are saying. Following this, we will offer biblical and historical support for the Left Behind view of the end times. In order to keep the book more reader-friendly, we have tried to put most of the technical information in endnotes. Feel free to take your time and read the endnotes as you go. We think the information there will help you understand the background for much of what we have to say.

Here are some of the major events we will consider in this book:

- the pretribulational Rapture
- the coming Russian/Islamic invasion of Israel
- the future seven-year Tribulation
- salvation during the Tribulation period
- the Antichrist
- 666—the mark of the beast
- the city of New Babylon

While Left Behind is a fictional series, we believe that the key events in the book are anything but fiction. In fact, this series proves the maxim that truth is stranger than fiction. Jenkins and LaHaye have told a story that has gripped and captivated a massive audience. But as incredible and enthralling as that story might be, the real events themselves—when they are unfolded in the end times—will eclipse anything people could imagine in their wildest dreams...or nightmares. We firmly believe that the basic end time events in the Left Behind series will transpire someday. Perhaps very soon.

A LEFT BEHIND COMPANION

It's very possible that many of you who have picked up this book don't really know much or care much about the criticism of Left

Behind. You've read the books, and all you want to do is take a more in-depth look at the truth behind the fiction. Maybe you would like to see the biblical evidence for the events in Left Behind laid out in a clear, easy-to-read format.

In either case—whether you have a strong interest in answering the Left Behind critics, or just want a concise primer on prophetic events—this book is for you. Our desire is for you to use this book as a kind of companion or support for the series. Our prayer is that God will use it to demonstrate and to confirm to the millions of faithful readers that the end time view presented in Left Behind is true, valid, and trustworthy. In other words, that it squares solidly with the Bible.

More than anything, we don't want the gripping, life-changing truth of the imminent, any-moment coming of Jesus Christ to get left behind.

So join us now, as we begin to look at *The Truth Behind Left Behind*. May God use it to give you greater confidence in Him, His Word, and His great plan for the end of this age...and the beginning of the next.

As you will see, this plan has already begun to unfold.

Great events are just ahead.

Perhaps closer than any of us have imagined.

CHAPTER TWO

THE RAPTURE

Left Behind

"WE *basically commiserated and wondered aloud what we were supposed to do next. Then somebody remembered Pastor's Rapture tape."*

"His what?" Chloe asked.

"Our senior pastor loved to preach about the coming of Christ to rapture his church, to take believers, dead and alive, to heaven before a period of tribulation on the earth. He was particularly inspired once a couple of years ago."

Rayford turned to Chloe. "You remember your mother talking about that. She was so enthusiastic about it."

"Oh yeah, I do."

"Well," Barnes said, "the pastor used that sermon and had himself videotaped in this office speaking directly to people who were left behind. He put it in the church library with instructions to get it out and play it if most everyone seemed to have disappeared. We all watched it a couple of times the other night. A few people wanted to argue with God, try to tell us that they really had been believers and should have been taken with the others, but we all knew the truth. We had been phony. There wasn't a one of us who didn't know what it meant to be a true Christian. We knew we weren't and that we had been left behind."

LEFT BEHIND, 194–195

The Left Behind theology is built upon a belief in the Rapture.

This is the conviction that in a moment of time, in the blink of an eye, every true believer in Jesus Christ will be physically transported up into the clouds to meet Jesus, then return with Him to His Father's house in heaven.

All this will happen within a split second of time and will occur before the onset of the horrifying seven-year Tribulation. At the same instant, the raptured believer will undergo the transformation of his or her current physical body into a new physical body, equipped to live forever with God in heaven. In conjunction with this astounding event will be the resurrection of all believers who have lived and died on earth within the two thousand years of the church age. They too will be given new bodies fit for heaven.

Both groups will meet Christ in the air and go to the Father's house in their new resurrection bodies to be with Jesus forever.

LEAVING THE RAPTURE BEHIND

Since the teaching of the Rapture is the linchpin in the Left Behind view of the end times, it's also at the center of criticism of the series. For the most part, critics of Left Behind don't even believe in a concept of the Rapture, and they certainly don't agree that it's taught in the Bible. In his book *Will Catholics Be "Left Behind"?* Carl Olson writes, "Although many biblical references are used to support it, the pre-Tribulational Rapture has no basis in Scripture."[1]

Gary DeMar, author of *End Times Fiction*, declares, "There is no single verse in the entire Bible that supports a pre-Trib Rapture."[2] Commenting on those who believe in the Rapture,

Paul Thigpen, author of *The Rapture Trap,* says, "Their cherished doctrine simply does not appear anywhere in the Bible."[3]

We strongly disagree with these statements. We believe that the Bible clearly teaches an event called the Rapture and that it will occur before the beginning of the seven-year Tribulation…just as it is presented in the Left Behind series.

But we don't want you to just take our word for it. Let's open the pages of Scripture together and take a closer look.

IS THE RAPTURE IN THE BIBLE?

If you were to read all of the 774,747 words (plus or minus) in any well-known English translation of the Bible, you would search in vain for the word *Rapture.* It isn't there. At the same time, however, you would also never encounter the words *Trinity, Bible,* or *grandfather.* And yet we know that all of these things are very real and true.

If, however, you happened to pick up a copy of the Latin Vulgate at a garage sale, produced by Jerome in the early 400s, you would indeed find the word *Rapture.* The Vulgate was the main Bible of the medieval Western church until the Reformation. It continues to this day as the primary Latin translation of the Roman Catholic church. It was Protestants, however, who introduced the word *Rapture* into the English language from the Latin *raeptius.*[4] And Jerome's Vulgate translated the original Greek verb *harpazô,* used by Paul under the inspiration of the Holy Spirit in 1 Thessalonians 4:17—where it is usually translated "caught up." One would think that Catholic critics of the Rapture, such as Carl Olson and Paul Thigpen, would take note of these things since the Vulgate was the Catholic Bible for almost fifteen hundred years.

The leading Greek Lexicon says that *harpazô* means "snatch, seize, i.e., take suddenly and vehemently."[5] This is the same meaning of the Latin word *rapio:* "to seize, snatch, tear away."[6] It should not be surprising to anyone that an English word in regular use today was developed from the Latin. That word, of course, is *rapture.*

Certainly the notion of a rapture appears many times in the Bible. English translators of the Bible could have been justified had they translated "caught up" in 1 Thessalonians 4:17 as the English word *rapture.* They also could have translated it with the word *snatch.* With no irreverence intended, we could just as easily and accurately call the Rapture "the Great Snatch."

Between the two authors of this book, we have at least fifty different commentaries on 1 Thessalonians in our libraries. Virtually all of them use *rapture* to describe the event in 1 Thessalonians 4:17. They do not appear interested in using it in a derogatory way; nor do any of them seem concerned that this word does not appear in English translations. In fact, most of these commentators do not hold to our rapture view. They merely use the word, acknowledging it as one of the many Latin words that have made it into the English theological vernacular. The bottom line? *Rapture* is a word commonly used within scholarly circles to describe the event recorded in 1 Thessalonians 4:17. There can be no doubt that the Greek word *harpazô* in this important passage, usually translated in English as "caught up," clearly conveys the rapture concept.

THREE KEY PASSAGES ON THE RAPTURE

The Rapture is referred to many times in the New Testament, but three main passages describe the Rapture of the church. Reading each of these passages will help you get a basic overview, directly from Scripture:

"Do not let your heart be troubled; believe in God, believe also in Me. In My Father's house are many dwelling places; if it were not so, I would have told you; for I go to prepare a place for you. If I go and prepare a place for you, I will come again and receive you to Myself, that where I am, there you may be also." (John 14:1–3)

Now I say this, brethren, that flesh and blood cannot inherit the kingdom of God; nor does the perishable inherit the imperishable. Behold, I tell you a mystery; we will not all sleep, but we will all be changed, in a moment, in the twinkling of an eye, at the last trumpet; for the trumpet will sound, and the dead will be raised imperishable, and we will be changed. For this perishable must put on the imperishable, and this mortal must put on immortality. But when this perishable will have put on the imperishable, and this mortal will have put on immortality, then will come about the saying that is written, "Death is swallowed up in victory. O death, where is your victory? O death, where is your sting?" The sting of death is sin, and the power of sin is the law; but thanks be to God, who gives us the victory through our Lord Jesus Christ. (1 Corinthians 15:50–57)

But we do not want you to be uninformed, brethren, about those who are asleep, so that you will not grieve as do the rest who have no hope. For if we believe that Jesus died and rose again, even so God will bring with Him those who have fallen asleep in Jesus. For this we say to you by the word of the Lord, that we who are alive and remain until the coming of the Lord, will not precede those who have fallen asleep. For the Lord Himself will descend from heaven with a shout, with the voice of the archangel and with the trumpet of God, and the dead in Christ will rise first. Then we who are alive and remain will be caught up together with them in the clouds to meet the Lord in the air, and so we shall always be with the Lord. Therefore comfort one another with these words. (1 Thessalonians 4:13–18)

TIMING IS EVERYTHING

Most evangelical Christians believe in the future event called the Rapture. But there is wide disagreement about the timing of this event in relation to the Tribulation period. Will the church go through any or all of the Tribulation before the Rapture occurs? In the minds of most believers, this is *the big question*—and the most hotly debated issue on the subject.

There are five main positions today on the timing of the Rapture:

1. *The Pre-Tribulation Rapture*: The Rapture will occur before the Tribulation period begins.
2. *The Mid-Tribulation Rapture*: The Rapture will occur at the midpoint of the Tribulation.
3. *The Post-Tribulation Rapture:* The Rapture will occur at the end of the Tribulation, right before the second coming of Christ back to earth. Believers will be caught up to meet Christ in the air and then immediately return with Him back to the earth.
4. *The Partial Rapture:* Faithful, devoted believers will be raptured before the Tribulation, but the rest of believers

will be left to go through the fiery purging of those days of judgment.

5. *The Pre-Wrath Rapture:* The Rapture will occur about three-fourths of the way (five and a half years) through the Tribulation, when the wrath of God begins to be poured out on the earth at the seventh seal (Revelation 6:17).

Of these five views, the two most commonly held today are pre-Trib and post-Trib.

VARIOUS VIEWS OF THE TIMING OF THE RAPTURE

1	**The Pretribulational Rapture**	The Rapture will occur before the Tribulation period begins.
2	**The Midtribulational Rapture**	The Rapture will occur at the midpoint of the Tribulation.
3	**The Posttribulational Rapture**	The Rapture will occur at the end of the Tribulation right before the second coming of Christ back to earth; believers will be raptured up to meet Christ in the air and then will return immediately with Him back to the earth.
4	**The Partial Rapture**	Faithful, devoted believers will be raptured before the Tribulation, but the rest of believers will be left to go through the purging of the Tribulation.
5	**The Prewrath Rapture**	The Rapture will occur about three-fourths (five and a half years) of the way through the Tribulation, when the wrath of God begins to be poured out on the earth at the seventh seal.

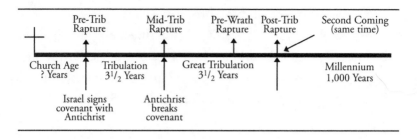

Clearly, the Left Behind series is built on the truth of the pre-Tribulation Rapture position. But is this view biblical? Reliable? Tenable?

Let's see.

MAKING THE CASE FOR THE PRE-TRIB VIEW

No single Bible verse says precisely, in so many words, when the Rapture will take place in relation to the Tribulation or the Second Coming. At least not in a way that would settle the issue to everyone's satisfaction. This does not mean, however, that the Bible waffles on this matter. It does not. As we shall see later, Scripture specifically promises that the church will *not* enter the time of God's wrath—another term for the Tribulation. Many biblical passages teach the pretribulational Rapture of the church.

We have to remember that many important biblical doctrines are not derived from a single verse, but come from a harmonization of several passages into systematic conclusions. Some truths are directly stated in the Bible, such as the deity of Christ (John 1:1; Titus 2:13). Other doctrines, like the Trinity and the incarnate nature of Christ, are the product of harmonizing the many passages that relate to these matters. Taking into account all that the Bible says on these issues, orthodox theologians, over time, concluded that God is a Trinity and that Christ is the God-man.

Similarly, a systematic, literal interpretation of all New Testament passages relating to the Rapture will lead to the pre-tribulational viewpoint—that at the Rapture, all living believers will be translated into heaven at least seven years before Christ's second coming.

This is what we believe the Bible teaches. And we say that with confidence.

While Dr. John Walvoord has presented *fifty* biblical arguments in favor of the pre-Trib Rapture, we will bring out only seven key points that favor this view as the most scriptural view on the timing of the Rapture.[7]

To facilitate memorizing these points, we have arranged them in a handy acronym that spells out the word PRETRIB.

- Place of the church in Revelation
- Removal of the restrainer
- Exemption from divine wrath
- Twenty-four elders
- Rapture of the church versus the return of Christ
- Imminence
- Blessed hope

Let's consider each of these seven points individually.

P—PLACE OF THE CHURCH IN REVELATION

The key passages in the New Testament that deal with the Tribulation period consistently fail to mention the presence of the church. The main section of the Bible that describes the Tribulation period is the fourteen chapters of Revelation 6–19, and this section is completely mute about the church.

In Revelation 1–3, the church is specifically mentioned nineteen times and is mentioned again in Revelation 22:16. But in Revelation 4–19, the church of Jesus Christ is strangely absent from the earth. The place of the church in the book of Revelation is evidence that the church will not be present on earth during the Tribulation.

R—REMOVAL OF THE RESTRAINER

Second Thessalonians 2 outlines and describes in broad terms three important ages that take us from the present age to eternity.

- *The present age*: the age of restraint (before the Rapture)
- *The tribulation age*: the age of rebellion (after the Rapture)
- *The messianic age*: the age of Revelation (after the Second Coming)

Amazingly, this present age in which we live is described as the time or age of *restraint*. That may not be a word you would have picked as a label for these days of cultural chaos. Even so, something or someone is restraining or holding back the full blast of evil that is to come when the Antichrist is finally unleashed.

Think about that for a moment.

If this evil world we live in now is described as a time of restraint, what in the world will it be like when the shackles are removed? What will this world be like when all restraint against the Antichrist and his wickedness is suddenly taken out of the way? It will be like removing a dam from a massive reservoir. Evil will overflow this world, swamping everything in its path.

The key question in this discussion is this: Who or what is this person or entity who—even at this moment—is restraining the appearance of Antichrist? Down through the centuries many candidates have been suggested. Here is a partial list:

- The Roman Empire
- The Jewish state
- The apostle Paul
- The preaching of the gospel
- Human government
- Satan
- Elijah
- Some unknown heavenly being
- Michael the archangel
- The Holy Spirit
- The church

St. Augustine was transparent concerning the restrainer when he said, "I frankly confess I do not know what He means." We can sympathize with Augustine, but we believe that several points help us identify this unnamed power.

1. The Greek word *katecho* ("what is holding him back," "the one who is holding it back" 2 Thessalonians 2:6–7) means to hold back or restrain.
2. The one who is holding back or restraining is both neuter and masculine: neuter "what is holding him back" (a principle); masculine "the one who is holding it back" (a person).
3. Whatever this restrainer is must be removable.
4. Finally, it must be powerful enough to hold back the outbreak of evil under Antichrist.

In answering these four questions, only one view is satisfactory. Just ask yourself this one thing: Who would be able to restrain evil and hold back the appearance of Antichrist? The answer of course is God. In this case it is God the Holy Spirit who is at work during this age in and through God's people, the church.

For these reasons, we believe the restrainer in 2 Thessalonians 2:6–7 is not just the Holy Spirit or just the church. Rather, the one holding back this vast tide of evil is God the Holy Spirit, present in the church of Jesus Christ. There are four strong reasons for making this identification:

1. This restraint requires omnipotent power.
2. This is the only view that adequately explains the change in gender in 2 Thessalonians 2:6–7. In Greek, the word *pneuma* (Spirit) is neuter. But the Holy Spirit is also consistently referred to by the masculine pronoun *He*—especially in John 14–16.
3. Scripture speaks of the Holy Spirit as the One who restrains evil—both in the world at large (Genesis 6:3), and in the heart of the believer (Galatians 5:16–17).
4. The church and its mission of proclaiming and portraying the gospel is the primary instrument the Holy Spirit uses to restrain evil in this age. We are the salt of the earth and the light of the world (Matthew 5:13–16). We are the temple of the Holy Spirit, both individually and corporately.

In summary, then, the influence and ministry of the Holy Spirit, indwelling and working through His people in this present age, is the power that holds back the dark flood of evil, which is ready to be released and sweep across our world. Barnhouse summarizes this view:

Well, what is keeping the Antichrist from putting in his appearance on the world stage? *You* are! You and every other member of the body of Christ on earth. The presence of the church of Jesus Christ is the restraining force that refuses to allow the man of lawlessness to be revealed. True, it is the Holy Spirit who is the real restrainer. But as both 1 Corinthians 3:16 and 6:19 teach, the Holy Spirit indwells the believer. The believer's body is the temple of the Spirit of God. Put all believers together then, with the Holy Spirit indwelling each of us, and you have a formidable restraining force.

For when the church is removed at the Rapture, the Holy Spirit goes with the church insofar as His restraining power is concerned. His work in this age of grace will be ended. Henceforth, during the Great Tribulation, the Holy Spirit will still be here on earth, of course—for how can you get rid of God?—but He will not be indwelling believers as He does now. Rather, He will revert to His Old Testament ministry of "coming upon" special people.[8]

When the Rapture occurs, the Spirit-indwelt church and its restraining influence will be removed, and Satan will put his plan into full swing by bringing his man onto center stage to take control of the world.

And it won't take long.

E—EXEMPTION FROM DIVINE WRATH

The Bible promises that God's people are exempt from the coming wrath of the Tribulation period (1 Thessalonians 1:9–10; 5:9;

Revelation 3:10). The nature of the entire Tribulation period is one of pounding judgment against a rebellious world. The judgment of God begins with the first seal that is opened in Revelation 6:1 and continues all the way until the Second Coming in Revelation 19:11–21. To say that God's wrath is confined to the very end of the Tribulation (as the Pre-Wrath view maintains), one must over-look the fact that all of the seal judgments are opened by the Lamb (Revelation 6:1). They are the wrath of God against sinful man, and they are opened at the very beginning of the Tribulation. The very nature and purpose of the entire Tribulation period demands that Christ's bride be caught away and delivered from this time of trouble.

Genesis 18–19, which records the rescue of Lot and his family from Sodom, clearly teaches that it is against God's character to destroy the righteous with the wicked when He pours out His judgment. The rapture of Enoch to heaven before the flood is another illustration of this principle (Genesis 5:24).

In Revelation 3:10–11a, the Lord's promise of deliverance from the Tribulation period is very specific. "Because you have kept the word of My perseverance, I also will keep you from the hour of testing, that hour which is about to come upon the whole world, to test those who dwell on the earth. I am coming quickly."

Notice two important things about this promise. First, the Lord promises to keep His people not just from the testing, but from the very *time* of worldwide testing. What is the time of worldwide testing? In the context of the book of Revelation, it is clearly the Tribulation period in chapters 6–19. Second, notice the means of this protection in verse 11: "I am coming quickly...."

Putting these two points together, it is clear that the Lord will protect His people from the time of worldwide testing by coming for them at the Rapture.

T—TWENTY-FOUR ELDERS

The book of Revelation includes twelve references to a group of individuals called "the twenty-four elders" (4:4, 10; 5:5, 6, 8, 11, 14; 7:11, 13; 11:16; 14:3; 19:4). The fact that they are mentioned twelve times makes them key players in Bible prophecy.

There are four main views concerning the identity of the twenty-four elders: 1) angelic beings, 2) Israel, 3) the church, and 4) all of the redeemed—Israel and the church. Seven key clues in Revelation reveal that the twenty-four elders represent the church, or the body of Christ.

- The title: They are called elders (*presbuteros*), who in Scripture are the representatives of God's people. We get our English word *Presbyterian* from this word. I am reminded of the little girl who came home from her Presbyterian Sunday school class, and her mother asked her what the lesson was about. The little girl replied, "We talked about heaven." "Well," her mother asked, "What did they say about it?" The little girl said, "The teacher told us that only twenty-four Presbyterians made it to heaven." (Hey, it's a joke). In the New Testament, the elders of a church are its representatives. These twenty-four elders represent the glorified church in heaven.
- The number: The Levitical priesthood in the Old Testament numbered in the thousands (1 Chronicles 24). Since all of the priests could not worship in the temple at the same time, the priesthood was divided into twenty-four groups. A representative of each group served in the temple on a rotating basis every two weeks. Though the nation of Israel was a kingdom of priests (Exodus 19:6),

only Aaron's sons were allowed to enter God's presence. In the church, however, *all* believers are priests unto God (1 Peter 2:5, 9). These twenty-four elders therefore are representative of the entire church of Jesus Christ.

- The position: They are seated on thrones. Enthronement with Christ is promised to the church (Revelation 3:21).
- The crowns: Angels are never pictured in Scripture wearing crowns, yet church age believers will receive crowns at the judgment seat of Christ (Revelation 2:10). These elders cannot include saved Israel because Old Testament believers will not be resurrected and rewarded until after the Tribulation is over (Daniel 12:1–3).
- The clothing: The white clothing of the elders is the clothing of the redeemed in the church age (Revelation 3:5, 18; 19:8).
- The praise: Only believers in the present church age can sing the song the elders sing in Revelation 5:9–10.
- The distinction: The elders are clearly distinguished from angels in Revelation 5:11.

Where are these elders? Are they on earth getting ready for the Tribulation? No! They are in heaven worshiping the Lamb and Him who sits on the throne. From their first mention in Revelation 4:4, the twenty-four elders are in heaven, judged, rewarded, and enthroned. Since the elders represent the church, this is another indication that the church must be raptured to heaven before the first judgment of the Tribulation is unleashed in Revelation 6:1. The only place you find the church in Revelation 4–19 is in heaven, represented by the twenty-four elders, who are seated on thrones, dressed in white, crowned with crowns, and worshiping the Lamb (Revelation 4:4, 10; 5:5, 6, 8, 11, 14).

R—RAPTURE OF THE CHURCH VERSUS THE RETURN OF
CHRIST

Some students of Bible prophecy strongly object to the notion that
the Rapture of the church and the return or Second Coming of
Christ are distinct events, separated by seven years. They contend
that this teaching claims two future comings of Christ when the
Bible presents only one such event.

But we believe that the Bible teaches two distinct phases or stages
for the coming of Christ: the Rapture and the Second Coming.

The Rapture is characterized in the New Testament as a "translation or resurrection coming" (1 Corinthians 15:51–52; 1
Thessalonians 4:15–17) in which the Lord comes *for* His church,
taking her to His Father's house (John 14:3). On the other hand,
Christ's Second Advent *with* His saints is described in Revelation
19, where He descends from heaven and arrives on earth to stay
and set up His messianic kingdom (Zechariah 14:4–5; Matthew
24:27–31). The differences between these two events are harmonized naturally by the pre-Trib position, while other views are not
able to comfortably account for such differences.

Here are some of the main verses that describe these two stages
of Christ's future coming.

RAPTURE	SECOND COMING
John 14:1–3	Daniel 2:44–45; 7:9–14; 12:1–3
Romans 8:19	Zechariah 12:10; 14:1–15
1 Corinthians 1:7–8; 15:51–53; 16:22	Matthew 13:41; 24:27–31; 26:64
Philippians 3:20–21; 4:5	Mark 13:14–27; 14:62
Colossians 3:4	Luke 17:20–37; 21:25–28
1 Thessalonians 1:10; 2:19; 4:13–18; 5:9, 23	Acts 1:9–11; 3:19–21
2 Thessalonians 2:1, 3	1 Thessalonians 3:13
	2 Thessalonians 1:6–10; 2:8

RAPTURE	SECOND COMING
1 Timothy 6:14	1 Peter 4:12–13
2 Timothy 4:1, 8	2 Peter 3:1–14
Titus 2:13	Jude 1:14–15
Hebrews 9:28	Revelation 1:7; 19:11–20:6; 22:7,
James 5:7–9	12, 20
1 Peter 1:7, 13; 5:4	
1 John 2:28–3:2	
Jude 1:21	
Revelation 2:15; 3:10	

The only real way to resolve this issue of whether the Rapture and the Second Coming are the same event is to set what the Bible says about these events side-by-side to see if they are describing the same occurrence.

You be the judge!

THE RAPTURE	THE RETURN (SECOND COMING)
Christ comes in the air (1 Thessalonians 4:16–17).	Christ comes to the earth (Zechariah 14:4).
Christ comes for His saints (1 Thessalonians 4:16–17).	Christ comes with His saints (1 Thessalonians 3:13; Jude 1:14).
Christ claims His bride.	Christ comes with His bride.
Not in the Old Testament (1 Corinthians 15:51).	Predicted often in the Old Testament.
There are no signs. It is imminent.	Portended by many signs (Matthew 24:4–29).
It is a time of blessing and comfort (1 Thessalonians 4:18).	It is a time of destruction and judgment (2 Thessalonians 2:8–12).

THE RAPTURE	THE RETURN (SECOND COMING)
Involves believers only (John 14:1–3; 1 Corinthians 15:51–55; 1 Thessalonians 4:13–18).	Involves all men (Matthew 24:1–25:46).
Only His own will see Him.	Every eye will see Him (Matthew 24:27; Revelation 1:7).
No reference to Satan.	Satan bound (Revelation 20:1–3).
Tribulation begins.	Millennium begins.
Christ comes as the Bright Morning Star.	Christ comes as the sun of righteousness (Malachi 4:2).

Dr. John Walvoord concludes that these "contrasts should make it evident that the translation of the church is an event quite different in character and time from the return of the Lord to establish His kingdom, and confirms the conclusion that the translation takes place before the Tribulation."[9]

Both events mention clouds, symbolizing a heavenly role in both, but other differences demonstrate that these are two distinct events. *To review…*

At the Rapture, the Lord comes *for* His saints (1 Thessalonians 4:16); at the Second Coming the Lord comes *with* His saints (1 Thessalonians 3:13).

At the Rapture, the Lord comes only for believers, but His return to the earth will impact all people.

The Rapture is a translation/resurrection event; the Second Coming is not.

At the Rapture, the Lord takes believers from earth to heaven "to the Father's house" (John 14:3). At the Second Coming, believers return from heaven to earth (Matthew 24:30). While both events describe a coming of the Lord, clearly they are not the same events because of the radical differences seen in the description of these occurrences. It is impossible to merge the Rapture and Second Coming into a single event that makes sense of the passages describing them.

The best harmonization of these two different events supports a pretribulational Rapture (which is signless and could happen at any moment), while the many events taking place during the Tribulation are best understood as signs leading up to the Second Coming.

I—IMMINENCE

The New Testament speaks of our Lord's return as imminent, meaning that it could happen at any moment. Other events *may* occur before an imminent event, but nothing else *must* take place before it happens. Imminency passages instruct believers to *look, watch,* and *wait* for His coming. Imminency means that Christ could come at any moment, although He may not come for two thousand years.

Here are some of the key New Testament passages that teach imminency:

- "…Awaiting eagerly the revelation of our Lord Jesus Christ" (1 Corinthians 1:7).
- "Maranatha" (1 Corinthians 16:22).
- "For our citizenship is in heaven, from which also we eagerly wait for a Savior, the Lord Jesus Christ" (Philippians 3:20).
- "The Lord is near" (Philippians 4:5).
- "…To wait for His Son from heaven" (1 Thessalonians 1:10).

- "Looking for the blessed hope and the appearing of the glory of our great God and Savior, Christ Jesus" (Titus 2:13).
- "So Christ...will appear a second time for salvation without reference to sin, to those who eagerly await Him" (Hebrews 9:28).
- "Therefore be patient, brethren, until the coming of the Lord.... for the coming of the Lord is near...behold, the Judge is standing right at the door" (James 5:7–9).
- "Fix your hope completely on the grace to be brought to you at the revelation of Jesus Christ" (1 Peter 1:13).
- "Waiting anxiously for the mercy of our Lord Jesus Christ to eternal life" (Jude 1:21).
- "I am coming quickly!" (Revelation 3:11; 22:7, 12, 20).
- "And the Spirit and the bride say, 'Come.' And let the one who hears say, 'Come.'...He who testifies to these things says, 'Yes, I am coming quickly.' Amen. Come, Lord Jesus" (Revelation 22:17, 20).

As we consider the passages above, we note that Christ may come at any moment—that the Rapture is actually imminent. Only the pretribulational view can give a full, literal meaning to such an any-moment event. Any other understanding of these passages must redefine imminence more loosely than these New Testament statements would allow. Dr. John Walvoord says, "The exhortation to look for 'the glorious appearing' of Christ to His own (Titus 2:13) loses its significance if the Tribulation must intervene first. Believers in that case should look for signs."[10]

Only the pre-Trib position allows for an imminent, any moment, signless coming of Christ for His own. Only those who believe in a pre-Trib Rapture can honestly sing, "Jesus may come today, glad day, glad day." For mid-Tribbers the Rapture must be at least three and a half years away, for pre-Wrathers it must be at least five and a half years away, and for post-Tribbers it is at least seven years down the road.

The any-moment coming of Christ is one of the truths in the New Testament that fills us with hope, anticipation, and motivation to godly living. Believers should live with this hope every day—the hope that Jesus may come today! Only the pre-Trib view gives full meaning to this hope.

B—BLESSED HOPE

The truth of the Rapture is intended to be a comfort and blessing to the Lord's people. It is our "blessed hope" (Titus 2:13). After describing the Rapture in 1 Thessalonians 4:18, Paul concludes with this injunction: "Therefore comfort one another with these words."

Just think about that sentence for a moment. If Paul taught a mid-Trib, pre-Wrath, or post-Trib Rapture, would the prospect of the Rapture really be that comforting? If God's people have to endure three and a half years, five and a half years, or all seven years of ghastly suffering before He comes, how much of a comfort would the Rapture be?

It wouldn't be a prospect that would immediately warm your heart!

The blessed hope of the Rapture is that Jesus will come and take us to be with Him forever *before* the time of worldwide devastation is unleashed. And what a comfort and blessing it is!

PIE IN THE SKY?

The pre-Tribulation Rapture is not just wishful "pie-in-the-sky, in the sweet-by-and-by" thinking. On the contrary, it is vitally connected to Christian living in the "nasty here-and-now." No wonder the early church coined the unique greeting of "Maranatha!" which reflected the primacy of the Blessed Hope as a very real presence in their everyday lives.

Maranatha literally means "Our Lord come!" (1 Corinthians 16:22). The life of the church today could only be improved if "Maranatha" were to return as a sincere greeting on the lips of an expectant people.

We have seen that the New Testament indeed teaches the Rapture of the church. We have also seen that this event will precede the seven-year Tribulation, just as it is pictured by Tim LaHaye and Jerry Jenkins in their Left Behind novels.

Remember, the timing of the Rapture is PRETRIB.

CHAPTER THREE

THE COMING RUSSIAN/ISLAMIC INVASION

Left Behind

FRUSTRATED *at their inability to profit from Israel's fortune and determined to dominate and occupy the Holy Land, the Russians had launched an attack against Israel in the middle of the night. The assault became known as the Russian Pearl Harbor.... The number of aircraft and warheads made it clear their mission was annihilation....*

Miraculously, not one casualty was reported in all of Israel. Otherwise Buck might have believed some mysterious malfunction had caused missile and plane to destroy each other. But witnesses reported that a firestorm, along with rain and hail and an earthquake, that consumed the entire offensive effort....

Editors and readers had their own explanations for the phenomenon, but Buck admitted, if only to himself, that he became a believer in God that day. Jewish scholars pointed out passages from the Bible that talked about God destroying Israel's enemies with a firestorm, earthquake, hail, and rain. Buck was stunned when he read Ezekiel 38 and 39 about a great enemy from the north invading Israel with the help of Persia, Libya, and Ethiopia.

LEFT BEHIND, 9–10, 13–15

One of the initial and key events of the end times as described in *Left Behind* is a massive surprise attack of Israel led by Russia. This invasion is detailed in a specific prophecy of the Old Testament prophet Ezekiel, written over twenty-five hundred years ago. That prophecy is found in Ezekiel 38–39.

These chapters describe a massive assault against Israel by a horde of nations in the "latter years" (Ezekiel 38:8). Ezekiel says that this invasion will occur at a time when Israel has been regathered from the nations and is living in peace and security (vv. 8, 14). As these nations mount their furious attack against Israel, it will appear that it's all over for the Jewish people. But at the last minute, God will intervene to miraculously deliver Israel from annihilation by destroying the invaders (vv. 18–22).

THE END OF DAYS

Detractors of the Left Behind view of the end times raise several issues concerning this view of Ezekiel 38–39.

First, some of them believe that this event occurred at some point in the distant past. In other words, they believe this particular prophecy has already been fulfilled. Gary DeMar, one of the foremost critics of the Left Behind theology, makes that contention. DeMar argues strenuously for a "literal" interpretation of Ezekiel 38–39 and repeatedly criticizes LaHaye and Jenkins for interpreting these chapters symbolically—thereby spiritualizing the text. In fact, DeMar insists that Ezekiel 38–39 was "literally" fulfilled by the events described in Esther 9, occurring in about 473 b.c. in the days of Queen Esther of Persia.[1] DeMar states that the parallels between the battles in Ezekiel 38–39 and Esther are "unmistakable."[2]

DeMar, however, fails to account for several striking differences between Ezekiel 38–39 and Esther 9. A simple reading of the two passages reveals that they cannot possibly be describing the same event.

Here are a few of the more apparent and problematic inconsistencies.

EZEKIEL 38–39	ESTHER 9
The land of Israel itself is invaded (38:16). The enemies fall on the mountains of Israel (39:4). Gog, the leader of the invasion, is buried in Israel (39:11).	Jews are attacked in cities throughout the Persian empire and defend themselves (9:2). The enemies die throughout the Persian empire.
The Jews bury the dead bodies over a period of seven months to cleanse the land of Israel (39:12).	No need to cleanse the land because the dead bodies aren't in Israel.
The invaders are destroyed by a massive earthquake in the land of Israel, infighting, plagues, and fire from heaven (38:19–22). God destroys the enemies supernaturally.	Attackers are killed by the Jewish people themselves, assisted by local government leaders (9:3–5).
Invaders are from as far west as ancient Put (modern Libya) (Ezekiel 38:5) and as far north as Magog, the land of the Scythians.	The Persian empire did not include these areas. It only extended as far west as Cush (modern Sudan) (Esther 8:9) and as far north as the bottom part of the Black and Caspian Seas.
God even sends fire upon Magog and those who inhabit the coastlands (39:6).	There is nothing even close to this in Esther 9.

One important question we might ask at this point is this: If Ezekiel 38–39 was literally fulfilled in the events of Esther 9, why did this escape the notice of everyone in Esther's day? Why isn't there any mention in Esther of this great fulfillment of Ezekiel's prophecy? And why aren't there any Jewish scholars in that day (or subsequently) who recognized this fulfillment?

The answer is quite clear. Esther 9 did not fulfill Ezekiel 38–39. In fact, an important Jewish holiday called Purim developed out of the Esther event (9:20–32). This is a joyous annual holiday to celebrate God's deliverance of Israel from the hand of her enemies. Purim's celebration includes the public reading of the book of Esther, but no tradition has developed or even been heard of in which the Jews read Ezekiel 38–39 in connection with this observance. If Ezekiel 38–39 had been a fulfillment of Esther, then no doubt a tradition of reading that passage would have arisen in conjunction with the celebration.

Fortunately, Ezekiel actually tells us when this invasion will occur. In Ezekiel 38:8, he says specifically that this invasion will occur in the "latter years." This is the only occurrence of this exact phrase in the Old Testament.

Another similar phrase occurs later in this chapter in verse 16: "It will come about in *the last days* that I shall bring you against My land" (italics added). This phrase is used in the Old Testament in reference to Israel's final time of distress or to Israel's final restoration to the messianic kingdom (see Isaiah 2:2; Jeremiah 23:20; 30:24; Hosea 3:5; Micah 4:1). Likewise, in Ezekiel 38:16, the phrase "in the last days" is a technical term that refers to the end times.[3] Therefore, Ezekiel is telling us that this invasion will occur in the final time of history in preparation for the establishment of the messianic kingdom of Christ.

Another very simple reason we can know that this invasion is still future is that nothing even remotely similar to the events in Ezekiel 38–39 has ever occurred in the past. Just think about it. When has Israel ever been invaded by all these nations listed in Ezekiel 38:1–6? Or when did God ever destroy an invading army like this with fire and brimstone from heaven, plagues, earthquakes, and infighting among the invaders (Ezekiel 38:19–22)?

The answer? Never. That's because Ezekiel is describing an invasion that is still future even in our day.

WEAPONS OF MASS DESTRUCTION?

Another point that critics of the Left Behind view often make is that the weapons mentioned in Ezekiel 38–39 are ancient weapons made out of wood—such as bows, arrows, shields, war clubs, and spears (39:9)—and that the means of transportation is horses (38:15).

Therefore, they conclude, if we truly take this passage literally, it has to be describing some ancient battle. Obviously it's difficult to envision a modern army using these weapons. Clearly horses, bows, arrows, shields, war clubs, and spears are mentioned in Ezekiel 38–39. If this is an end-time invasion as Left Behind presents it, then it is very doubtful that these exact weapons will be used. Rather, their modern counterparts will be used.

Inspired by the Holy Spirit, Ezekiel spoke in language that the people of his day could understand. If he had spoken of MIG-29s, laser-fired missiles, tanks, and assault rifles, this text would have been nonsensical to everyone until the twentieth century. For that matter, the main point of Ezekiel's great prophecy is that a specific group of nations will attack Israel, intent on completely destroying her. The focus clearly is *not* the specific weapons that will be used by these invaders. The point is that weapons of destruction will be employed and that there will be all-out warfare. This is not "symbolic interpretation" as DeMar alleges, but rather under-standing God's Word in its historical context—as it would have been understood by the original audience. The Holy Spirit speaks to people in their own context and culture in ways that commu-nicate God's truth in a meaningful, understandable way.

In a related issue, nine specific ancient nations are mentioned in Ezekiel 38:1–6. All of these nations and their ancient geo-graphical territories are mentioned in the Table of Nations in Genesis 10. Just as with the weapons, these exact nations under these specific ancient names will not attack Israel because they no longer exist under the names listed in that passage. You will scan your world atlas in vain for the nations of Rosh, Gomer, Magog, Meshech, Togarmah, or Put. The names of some of these areas have changed numerous times through the millennia. *But the modern nations that inhabit the same geographical territory as these ancient peoples and nations will invade Israel.* Again, the Holy Spirit speaks to people in language they can grasp. He used the ancient names of these places, going all the way back to Genesis 10 to clearly identify the geographical areas that will invade Israel in the end times.

The following chart will help show how Ezekiel used ancient weapons and places people in his own day could understand—and that we can still apply twenty-five hundred years later.

EZEKIEL 39–39	END TIME FULFILLMENT
Ancient weapons that are no longer used by civilized nations.	Modern weapons that correspond to the ancient weapons.
Ancient nations that no longer exist under the names in Ezekiel.	Contemporary counterparts in the same geographical locations.

ARE THE RUSSIANS COMING?

The third main point that opponents of the Left Behind theology raise concerning Ezekiel 38–39 is the involvement of Russia in the invasion.

Ezekiel 38–39 predicts an invasion of the land of Israel in the last days by a vast confederation of nations from north of the Black and Caspian Seas, extending down to modern Iran in the east, and as far as modern Libya to the west. The leader of this offensive is called Gog, who is identified as the prince of Rosh, Meshech, and Tubal.

In *Left Behind,* Rosh is portrayed as Russia.

But is this identification valid? Is this prophecy a reference to the nation we know today as Russia?

Those who oppose the Left Behind theology state with great certainty that there is no way that the word *Rosh* in Ezekiel 38–39 could have any possible connection to modern Russia.[4]

Let's look at the biblical and historical evidence to see if this criticism is justified.

A DESCRIPTION...OR A NAME?

The first point that must be considered is whether the word *Rosh* in Ezekiel 38:2–3 and 39:1 is a proper name or simply an adjective.

The word *Rosh* in Hebrew simply means head, top, summit, or chief. It is a very common word and is used in all Semitic languages, occurring approximately 750 times in the Old Testament, along with its roots and derivatives.

The problem is that the word *Rosh* in Ezekiel can be translated as either a proper noun *or* an adjective. Many translations take *Rosh* as an adjective and translate it as "chief." The *King James Version, Revised Standard Version, New American Bible,* and the *New International Version* all adopt this translation. However the *Jerusalem Bible, New*

English Bible, and *New American Standard Bible* all translate *Rosh* as a proper name indicating a geographical location.[5]

The weight of evidence favors taking *Rosh* as a proper name. Five arguments favor this view.

First, the eminent Hebrew scholars C. F. Keil and Wilhelm Gesenius both hold that the better translation of Rosh in Ezekiel 38:2–3 and 39:1 is as a proper noun referring to a specific geographical location.[6]

Second, the Septuagint, which is the Greek translation of the Old Testament, translates *Rosh* as the proper name *Ros.* This is especially significant since the Septuagint was translated only three centuries after Ezekiel was written (obviously much closer to the original than any modern translation).[7] The mistranslation of Rosh in many modern translations as an adjective can be traced to the Latin Vulgate of Jerome.[8]

Third, many Bible dictionaries and encyclopedias in their articles on Rosh support taking it as a proper name in Ezekiel 38. Some examples: *New Bible Dictionary, Wycliffe Bible Dictionary,* and *International Standard Bible Encyclopedia.*

Fourth, Rosh is mentioned the first time in Ezekiel 38:2 and is then repeated in 38:3 and 39:1. If Rosh were simply a title, it would probably be dropped in these two places; when titles are repeated in Hebrew, they are generally abbreviated.

Fifth, the most impressive evidence in favor of taking Rosh as a proper name is simply that this translation is the most accurate. G. A. Cooke, a Hebrew scholar, translates Ezekiel 38:2: "the chief of Rosh, Meshech and Tubal." He calls this "the most natural way of rendering the Hebrew."[9]

Having established that Rosh should be taken as a proper name of a geographical area, the next task is to determine what geographical location is in view.

IS ROSH RUSSIA?

One of the main charges against those who identify Rosh as Russia is that we do this only because the two words sound alike.[10] On a *Bible Answer Man* radio broadcast in October 2002, the host, Hank Hannegraaf, asked Gary DeMar what he thought about Tim LaHaye identifying Rosh as Russia, since the two words sound so much alike. DeMar responded, "The idea that you can take a word in Hebrew that sounds like the word in English, and then go with that and to create an entire eschatological position based upon that is…it's nonsense."

The problem is that DeMar's argument is a flimsy straw man. Our view that Rosh in Ezekiel 38–39 is Russia is *not* based on the fact that the two words sound alike. We agree that this is not an acceptable method of biblical interpretation.

There are two substantial reasons for identifying ancient Rosh with modern Russia. First, Wilhelm Gesenius, who died in 1842 and is considered by modern Hebrew scholars as one of the greatest scholars of the Hebrew language, unquestionably believed that Rosh in Ezekiel was a proper noun identifying Russia. Gesenius says that *Rosh* in Ezekiel 38:2–3; 39:1 is a "northern nation, mentioned with Meshech and Tubal; undoubtedly the *Russians,* who are mentioned by the Byzantine writers of the tenth century, under the name *the Ros,* dwelling to the north of Taurus…as dwelling on the river Rha (*Wolga*)."[11]

This identification by Gesenius cannot be passed off lightly. Gesenius, as far as we know, was not a pretribulationalist or even a premillennialist. He had no eschatological, end time ax to grind. Yet objectively he says without hesitation that Rosh in Ezekiel 38–39 is Russia.[12]

Second, there is considerable historical evidence that a place known as Rosh was very familiar in the ancient world. While the word has a variety of forms and spellings, it is clear that the same people are in view.

In Egyptian inscriptions, Rosh (Rash) is identified as a place that existed as early as 2600 B.C. There is a later Egyptian inscription from about 1500 B.C. that refers to a land called Reshu that was located to the north of Egypt.[13]

The place-name Rosh (or its equivalent in the respective languages) is found at least twenty times in other ancient documents. It is found three times in the Septuagint, ten times in Sargon's inscriptions, once in Assurbanipal's cylinder, once in Sennacherib's annals, and five times in Ugaritic tablets.[14]

Clearly, Rosh was a well-known place in Ezekiel's day. In the sixth century B.C., the time when Ezekiel wrote his prophecy, several bands of the Rosh people lived in an area to the north of the Black Sea. Many scholars have traced a direct connection between these people and the people from which Russia derives its name. Jon Ruthven, after an in-depth investigation into the issue, says:

> But other indications, such as geographical location, ethnography, and the general descriptions of the culture, provide us with some confidence that there is a direct connection between the *Rosh* of Ezekiel and the tribal Rus from which the modern Russia derives its name. Indeed this is the suggestion of one Russian historian, who states: "The first reference to the…*Russ*, the ancestors of the Russian rulers, is found in Ezekiel 38:2f."[15]

After providing extensive, overwhelming evidence of the origin and early history of the Rosh people, and then tracing them through the centuries, Clyde E. Billington Jr. concludes:

Historical, ethnological, and archaeological evidence all
favor the conclusion that the Rosh people of Ezekiel
38–39 were the ancestors of the Rus/Ros people of
Europe and Asia…. The Rosh people who are mentioned in Ezekiel 38–39 were well-known to ancient and
medieval writers by a variety of names which all derived
from the names of Tiras and Rosh…. Those Rosh
people who lived to the north of the Black Sea in
ancient and medieval times were called the
Rus/Ros/Rox/Aorsi from very early times…. From this
mixture with Slavs and with the Varangian Rus in the
9th century, the Rosh people of the area north of the
Black Sea formed the people known today as the
Russians.[16]

"MANY PEOPLES WITH YOU"

In the last days, when Russia pushes down into Israel from the
north, she will be led by a power-crazed madman named Gog.
Mentioned eleven times in Ezekiel 38–39, the word *Gog* is not a
name, but a title, like Pharaoh, Caesar, or President. Gog means a
high mountain, high, supreme, or a height. He is also called a
prince (38:2; 39:1).

Gog, the leader of Russia, will be joined by a host of allies.
Ezekiel 38:9 refers to "You and your allies—a vast and awesome
horde." Nine specific geographical locations are mentioned in
Ezekiel 38:1–6. As we have mentioned, Ezekiel used ancient place-
names that would be familiar to the people of his day. While the
names of these places may change over time, the geographical territory stays the same.

ANCIENT NAME	MODERN NATION
Magog (Ancient Scythians)	**Modern Central Asia** (Islamic republics of the former Soviet Union)
Meshech (Ancient Muschki and Musku in Cilicia and Cappadocia)	Turkey
Tubal (Ancient Tubalu in Cappadocia)	Turkey
Persia (Name changed to Iran in 1935)	Iran
Ethiopia (Ancient Cush, south of Egypt)	Sudan
Put (Ancient nation west of Egypt)	Libya
Gomer (Ancient Cimmerians—from seventh century to first century B.C. in central/western Anatolia)	Turkey
Beth-togarmah (Til-garimmu—between ancient Carchemish and Haran)	**Southern Turkey**[17]

From this list, it seems that Russia will have five key allies: Turkey, Iran, Libya, Sudan, and the nations of Central Asia. Amazingly, all of these nations are Muslim nations—and Iran, Libya, and Sudan are three of Israel's most ardent opponents. Iran is one of the "axis of evil" nations, trying so desperately to develop a nuclear weapons program. Many of these nations are hotbeds of militant Islam and are either forming or strengthening their ties as these words are being written. This list of nations reads like the Who's Who of this week's newspaper.

It certainly doesn't take a very active imagination to envision these nations conspiring together to invade Israel in the near future.

CONCLUSION

The Left Behind view of a massive invasion of Israel in the end times led by Russia is not "fiction." It is supported by cogent biblical, grammatical, and historical evidence. Based on what we have seen, we can legitimately draw four simple conclusions.

1. No event in Israel's past history since the time of Ezekiel's prophecy even comes close to fitting the details of Ezekiel 38–39 (especially Esther 9). Therefore, since we believe that the prophecy must be literally fulfilled, it must still be future even in our day.
2. The grammar of the Hebrew Bible supports the translation of Rosh as a proper noun denoting a geographical location.
3. Historical evidence points to a people in ancient and medieval times called the Rus/Ros/Rox who lived in the area of modern Russia. This people group can be historically traced and identified with the people called Rosh in Ezekiel 38–39.
4. Ezekiel 38–39 describes a future end-time invasion of Israel by Russia and many allies (all of whom today are Islamic nations that despise Israel).

The Russians are indeed coming—in one all-out attempt to crush God's chosen people and grab God's ancient land. When the smoke clears, however, it will be the attackers who find themselves crushed.

And this time Israel won't have to fire a shot.

CHAPTER FOUR

ISRAEL: GOD'S SUPER SIGN

Tribulation Force

TO say arbitrarily, *Pontifex Maximus Peter wrote in an official Enigma Babylon declaration,* that the Jewish and Protestant Bible, containing only the Old and New Testaments, is the final authority for faith and practice, represents the height of intolerance and disunity. It flies in the face of all we have accomplished, and adherents to that false doctrine are hereby considered heretics.

Pontifex Maximus Peter had lumped the Orthodox Jews and the new Christian believers together. He had as much problem with the newly rebuilt temple and its return to the system of sacrifices as he did with the millions and millions of converts to Christ. And ironically, the supreme pontiff had strange bedfellows in opposing the new temple. Eli and Moishe, the now world-famous witnesses whom no one dared oppose, often spoke out against the temple. But their logic was an anathema to Enigma Babylon.

"Israel has rebuilt the temple to hasten the return of their Messiah," Eli and Moishe had said, "not realizing that she built it apart from the true Messiah, who has already come! Israel has constructed a temple of rejection! Do not wonder why so few of the 144,000 Jewish evangelists are

from Israel! Israel remains largely unbelieving and will soon suffer for it!"

TRIBULATION FORCE, 401–402

The regathering of the Jewish people to the land of Israel is an essential element in the Left Behind view of the end times. Just think about it. Almost every important event in this landmark series hinges on the existence of the nation of Israel.

Russia and her Arab/Islamic allies invade the Jewish people in the land of Israel.

The Jewish temple is rebuilt on the temple mount in Jerusalem.

The Antichrist, Nicolae Carpathia, makes his seven-year treaty with the nation of Israel—later breaking the pact, invading Israel, and desecrating the temple.

Up in northern Israel, at Armageddon, all the nations of the earth gather to come against Israel and eradicate the Jewish people once and for all.

For those who hold to the Left Behind view of coming events, the regathered nation of Israel truly is the "super sign" of the end times.

We believe, therefore, that the dispersion of the Jewish people by the Romans in A.D. 70, their preservation as an ethnically distinct people during the nineteen hundred years of their scattering, and their regathering to form the modern state of Israel is a miracle brought about by the hand of God. The current state of Israel is prophetically important because the Jewish people have been regathered in order to fulfill events during the coming seven-year Tribulation period, following the Rapture.

At least that's what those of us who hold to the Left Behind theology believe the Bible teaches. It's not surprising to learn that critics of that view strongly disagree. Gary North has boasted that he has a book already in his computer for when "Israel gets pushed into the sea, or converted to Christ."[1] Lutheran Don Matzat has said:

> The present-day nation of Israel is no more involved in God's plans for the future than is France, England, Germany, the United States, etc. The teaching of the New Testament is very clear—Jesus fulfilled everything pertaining to Israel and formed the New Israel.[2]

Following the same train of thought as Matzat, Left Behind critic Gary DeMar adds:

> According to LaHaye, the "super sign" is related to the national status of Israel in the twentieth century....
>   Where is this "super sign" found in the Bible? Not in the New Testament. There is not a single verse in the entire New Testament that says anything about Israel becoming a nation again. Nothing prophetic in the New Testament depends on Israel becoming a nation again. If Israel becoming a nation again is such "a significant sign," then why doesn't the New Testament specifically mention it?[3]

Since the Left Behind theology is based upon what the Bible teaches about Israel and the end times, we will now turn to that infallible source to see what it says about a future for Israel.

MODERN ISRAEL IS A WORK OF GOD

Those who say that modern Israel has no more prophetic significance than France completely ignore a very significant fact. Israel is mentioned *thousands* of times throughout Scripture. And France? Not at all, of course.

What's more, the Bible insists many times over that *Israel is not finished in history.* Speaking of the Jewish people, Paul said in Romans 11:1: "I say then, God has not rejected His people, has He? May it never be!"

Gary DeMar cannot find a New Testament promise of Israel's future restoration. Yet we have just cited a strong, biblical assertion—"May it never be!"—that God has not rejected Israel. Since we believe that all sixty-six books of the Bible are equally inspired and infallible, then Old Testament statements of Israel's national restoration will do just fine. What DeMar and any opponent of the Left Behind theology must come up with is any single biblical passage that teaches that God is forever finished with His chosen people. In fact, Romans 11:1 says just the opposite.

To gain some further insight into God's future program for the nation of Israel, let's go back to that nation's beginning and trace what God has to say about the Jewish people and the land He gave them.

GOD ALWAYS KEEPS HIS WORD

The Lord called Abram out of Ur of the Chaldeans and made an unconditional covenant, or contract, with him. This contract, known as the Abrahamic covenant, contained three major provisions: 1) a land to Abram and Israel, 2) a seed or physical descendants of Abraham, and 3) a worldwide blessing (Genesis 12:1–3).

In order to make His point clear, the Lord put Abram to sleep and made Himself the only signatory of the contract (Genesis 15:1–21). God told Abram, "To your descendants I have given this land" (v. 18). This covenant is repeated to Abraham, Isaac, Jacob, and their descendants about twenty-five times in the book of Genesis. God's promise to the patriarchs is said to be an everlasting covenant (17:7, 13, 19).

The book of Deuteronomy says at least twenty-five times that the land is a gift to the people of Israel from the Lord (1:20, 25; 2:29; 3:20; 4:40; 5:16, etc.). Walter Kaiser notes that "sixty-nine times the writer of Deuteronomy repeated the pledge that Israel would one day 'possess' and 'inherit' the land promised to her."[4]

Deuteronomy 28–30 lays out the conditions for Israel to experience blessing within the land. We must remember that while the land was given unconditionally to the people of Israel, the Mosaic law provides subconditions for enjoying God's blessings in the land. The Tribulation period will be a time of divine discipline on the nation, bringing about Israel's repentance and obedience. And then, during those grand and golden days of the millennial kingdom, she will experience full occupation of her land, reaping the many blessings promised in the Old Testament.

Throughout the Old Testament the prophets convict Israel for her disobedience, but always with a view toward a future restoration, when Israel will dwell in peace and prosperity (Isaiah 11:1–9; 12:1–3; 27:12–13; 43:1–8; 66:20–22; Jeremiah 16:14–16; 30:10–11; 31:31–37; Ezekiel 11:17–21; 34:11–16; 39:25–29; Hosea 1:10–11; Joel 3:17–21; Amos 9:11–15; Micah 4:4–7; Zephaniah 3:14–20; Zechariah 8:4–8; 10:8–12).

It is important to note that Zechariah wrote his great prophecy *after* the return from the Babylonian captivity, and yet…he speaks of a *future* restoration to the land. What the prophet plainly indicates is that Israel's past restorations did *not* ultimately fulfill the land promise given to Abraham, Isaac, and Jacob.

Speaking through the psalmist, the Lord declares: "For the LORD has chosen Zion; He has desired it for His habitation. 'This

is My resting place forever; Here I will dwell, for I have desired it'"
(Psalm 132:13–14).

We believe that this statement is still in effect to this very hour
since nowhere in the Bible has the Lord revoked any of His promises to His people. The Left Behind view of the end times believes,
consistent with God's plan as stated in the pages of Scripture, in a
glorious future for national Israel.

TWO END-TIME REGATHERINGS

To properly understand the end-time homecoming or regathering
of the Jews to their promised land, we need to keep five major
points in mind. Let's look briefly at each of these five points and
see what the Bible says.

1. THE BIBLE PREDICTS THAT ISRAEL WILL EXPERIENCE TWO WORLDWIDE, END-TIME REGATHERINGS TO THE PROMISED LAND.

Dozens of biblical passages predict this global event. It is a common mistake, however, to lump all of these passages into one
fulfillment time frame, especially in relation to the modern state of
Israel. Modern Israel is prophetically significant and is certainly fulfilling Bible prophecy. But when we read God's Word, we need to
be careful to distinguish which verses are being fulfilled in our day
and which await future fulfillment.

In short, there will be two (and only two) end-time regatherings: one before the Tribulation and one after the Tribulation. The
first worldwide regathering will be a return in unbelief, in preparation for the judgment of the Tribulation. The second worldwide
regathering will be a return in faith at the end of the Tribulation,

in preparation for the blessing of the Millennium, or thousand-year reign of Christ.[5]

One important passage that deals with Israel's two regatherings is Isaiah 11:11–12:

> Then it will happen on that day that the Lord will again recover *the second time* with His hand the remnant of His people, who will remain, from Assyria, Egypt, Pathros, Cush, Elam, Shinar, Hamath, and from the islands of the sea. And He will lift up a standard for the nations and assemble the banished ones of Israel, and will gather the dispersed of Judah from the four corners of the earth. (Italics added.)

The return in Isaiah 11 clearly refers to the final worldwide regathering of Israel in faith, at the climax of the Tribulation, and in preparation for the millennial kingdom. Isaiah specifically says that this final regathering is the second one. That, of course, raises the obvious question: When did the first regathering occur?

Some maintain that the first return is the Babylonian return from exile that began in about 536 B.C. But how could this return be described as *worldwide*, as set forth in Isaiah 11?[6]

The only reasonable conclusion, then, is that the first international regathering must be the one in preparation for the Tribulation.

Arnold Fruchtenbaum writes:

> The entire context is Isaiah 11:11–12:6. In this context, he is speaking of the final worldwide regathering in faith in preparation for blessing. Isaiah numbers the final worldwide regathering in faith in preparation of the

Messianic Kingdom as the *second* one. In other words, the last one is only the second one. If the last one is the second one, how many can there be before that? Only one. The first one could not have been the return from Babylon since that was not an international regathering from the four corners of the world, only a migration from one country (Babylonia) to another (Judea). The Bible does not allow for several worldwide regatherings in unbelief; it allows for *one* worldwide regathering in unbelief, followed by the last one, the one in faith, which is the second one. This text only permits two worldwide regatherings from *the four corners of the earth*. Therefore, the present Jewish State *is* very relevant to Bible prophecy.[7]

This chart provides a quick visual comparison and contrast between Israel's two great regatherings.[8]

THE PRESENT (FIRST) REGATHERING	THE PERMANENT (SECOND) REGATHERING
Worldwide	Worldwide
Return to part of the land	Return to all the land
Return in unbelief	Return in faith
Restored to the land only	Restored to the land and the Lord
Man's work (secular)	God's work (spiritual)
Sets the stage for the Tribulation (discipline)	Sets the stage for the Millennium (blessing)

Here are some of the key Scripture verses related to each of these regatherings:

ISRAEL—Regathered Before the Tribulation in Unbelief (Current State of the Nation)	ISRAEL—Regathered Before the Millennium in Belief (Future State)
Ezekiel 20:33–38; 22:17–22; 36:22–24 Isaiah 11:11–12 Zephaniah 2:1–2 Ezekiel 38–39	Deuteronomy 4:29–31; 30:1–10 Isaiah 27:12–13; 43:5–7 Jeremiah 16:14–15; 31:7–10 Ezekiel 11:14–18 Amos 9:14–15 Zechariah 10:8–12 Matthew 24:31

FIRST WORLDWIDE GATHERING IN UNBELIEF

2. THE FIRST WORLDWIDE REGATHERING, IN UNBELIEF, WILL SET THE STAGE FOR THE EVENTS OF THE TRIBULATION PERIOD.

When the modern state of Israel was born in 1948, it not only became an important stage-setting development, but also began an actual fulfillment of specific Bible prophecies about an international regathering of the Jews in unbelief before the judgment of the Tribulation. The following Old Testament passages predict this development: Ezekiel 20:33–38; 22:17–22; 36:22–24; 37:1–14; Isaiah 11:11–12; Zephaniah 2:1–2.

Zephaniah 2:1–2 says that there will be a worldwide regathering of Israel before the Day of the Lord, which we commonly call the Tribulation period: "Gather yourselves together, yes, gather, O nation without shame, before the decree takes effect—the day passes like the chaff—before the burning anger of the LORD comes upon you, before the day of the LORD's anger comes upon you."

Ezekiel 20:33–38 sets forth a regathering that must take place before the Tribulation. The passage speaks of bringing the nation of Israel back "from the peoples and gather you from the lands where you are scattered, with a mighty hand and with an outstretched arm and with wrath poured out" (v. 34). "With wrath poured out" is a descriptive reference to the Tribulation. In order for this to occur in history, Israel must be back in the land before the Tribulation. This passage distinctly teaches that it is the Lord who is bringing them back, and the current nation of Israel is in the process of fulfilling this passage.

In a similar vein, two chapters later, Ezekiel receives yet another revelation about a future regathering of national Israel (22:17–22). This time the Lord is "going to gather you into the midst of Jerusalem" (v. 19). Like a skilled metalworker, the Lord will use the fire of the Tribulation to purge out the unfaithful. The Lord is going to "gather you [Israel] and blow on you with the fire of My wrath, and you will be melted in the midst of it" (v. 21). Once again, "My wrath" depicts the time of the Tribulation. It also follows here that the nation must be regathered before that event can take place. The outcome of this event will be that the nation "will know that I, the LORD, have poured out My wrath on you" (v. 22).

Before these things can happen, Jews from all over the world must return to the land, just as we see happening with the modern state of Israel. This, of course, doesn't mean that *every* Jew in the world has to be back in the land. But it does clearly mean that many of the Jewish people must have returned to their ancient homeland. End-time prophecy in Scripture is built upon the assumption that Israel is both regathered to her land and is functioning as a nation.

The implications of Daniel 9:27 are unmistakable. "And he [Antichrist] will make a firm covenant with the many for one week [one week of years or seven years]." In other words, the seven-year Tribulation period will begin with the signing of a covenant between Antichrist and the leaders of Israel. Obviously, the signing of this treaty presupposes the presence of a Jewish leadership in a Jewish nation. This Jewish state must exist before a treaty can be signed.[9]

To summarize, then, the logic goes like this: The Tribulation can't begin until the seven-year covenant is signed. The covenant can't be signed until a Jewish state exists. Therefore, a Jewish state must exist before the Tribulation.

In view of all this, we believe that the main purpose for the regathering of Israel relates directly to the peace pact with Antichrist, as described in Daniel 9:27. For such a treaty to be viable, the Jews have to be present in the land and organized into a political state. And since 1948 *they have been.* It is this modern miracle—something unheard of in history—that we, our parents, and our grandparents have witnessed unfolding before our eyes. An ancient and scattered people have returned to their ancestral homeland after almost two millennia, making the peace covenant of Daniel 9:27 possible for the first time since A.D. 70.[10]

As a result, the stage is set for the very event that will trigger the Great Tribulation and usher in the final days of the world as we know it. Much to the disappointment of those who are opposed to the Left Behind theology, the modern state of Israel is in just such a position. This truly constitutes a super sign for the end times.

A GATHERING IN STAGES

3. THE BIBLE PREDICTS THAT ISRAEL'S FIRST REGATHERING BEFORE THE TRIBULATION WILL OCCUR IN PHASES OR STAGES.

In A.D. 70, the land of Israel, the city of Jerusalem, and the Jewish temple were crushed under the heel of Roman domination. Since that time, the Jews have been spread out all over the world.

God's warning of worldwide exile in Deuteronomy 28:64–66 has been literally, graphically fulfilled in the last nineteen hundred years:

> Moreover, the LORD will scatter you among all peoples, from one end of the earth to the other end of the earth; and there you shall serve other gods, wood and stone, which you or your fathers have not known. Among those nations you shall find no rest, and there will be no resting place for the sole of your foot; but there the LORD will give you a trembling heart, failing of eyes, and despair of soul. So your life shall hang in doubt before you; and you will be in dread night and day, and shall have no assurance of your life.

But as we have seen, the Bible predicts that Israel will return to the land in the end times. Scripture further indicates that this regathering will occur in stages.

In the famous "valley of dry bones" vision of Ezekiel 37:1–14, the bones symbolize the nation of Israel coming back together in the end times. In that passage, Ezekiel sees a graveyard vision illustrating the national return, restoration, and regeneration of "the whole house of Israel" (v. 11). Israel is first restored physically, and that restoration is pictured as bones, sinew, and skin coming together. The complete skeleton comes together bone by bone. Joint by joint. But it is still a lifeless corpse (v. 8). Ezekiel calls this a work of the Lord (v. 14). If, as we believe, this word picture portrays the modern state of Israel, then this regathering since 1948 has certainly been a work of God and is biblically significant.

Following this, Ezekiel witnesses Israel's spiritual regeneration, as the Spirit breathes spiritual life into the dead nation (v. 9). Of course, this spiritual regeneration won't occur until Messiah returns.

We believe that the process of physical regathering to the Land has begun. Preparations for the first worldwide regathering of Israel have been going on for about 130 years now. A pile of bones is beginning to come together and take shape.

Let's consider what has happened so far.

The modern beginning of the return to the land goes back as early as 1871, when a few pioneering Jews began to trickle back. By 1881, about twenty-five thousand Jews had settled there. At the first Zionist congress in 1897, led by Theodore Herzl, the goal of reclaiming the land for the Jewish people was officially adopted. The process, however, was agonizingly slow. By 1914, only eighty thousand Jews had moved into the land.

During World War I, the British sought support from the Jews for the war effort. On November 2, 1917, British Foreign Secretary Arthur J. Balfour issued what has become known as the Balfour Declaration. The declaration was stated in a letter from Balfour to Lord Rothschild, a wealthy Jewish entrepreneur. In the letter, Secretary Balfour gave approval to the Jewish goal of reclamation: "His Majesty's Government views with favor the establishment in Palestine of a national home for the Jewish people...."

In the face of persistent Arab pressure, however, and the desire of the British to maintain friendly relations with the Arabs, little was done in pursuit of the Balfour Declaration. Even so, it fanned into flame Jewish hopes for the establishment of a homeland in the Holy Land—and encouraged more Jews to return. By 1939, when World War II broke out, about 450,000 Jews had managed to return to their homeland.

The second world war and Nazi Germany's heinous, despicable treatment of the Jewish people created worldwide sympathy and a favorable environment for the Jewish people. Hitler's atrocities actually provided the greatest momentum for the establishment of a national homeland for the Jews. With United Nations approval, British control of the land ended on May 14, 1948—and a nation was reborn. At that time, Israel was given five thousand square miles of territory and had a population of 650,000 Jews and several hundred thousand Arabs.

Since that historic day, further waves of immigrants have poured into Israel from all over the world, most notably from Ethiopia and the Soviet Union. By 2002, 37 percent of the 13.2 million Jews in the world were back in the land of Israel. To put this in perspective, in 1948 only 6 percent of the Jews in the world were in Israel. It is estimated that by the year 2030, half of the Jews worldwide will be back in the land.

And it is happening before our very eyes.

THE FINAL SCATTERING

4. THE JEWISH PEOPLE WILL BE SCATTERED FOR THE FINAL TIME DURING THE PERSECUTION OF THE ANTICHRIST.

During the Tribulation period, the Jewish people will be scattered over the face of the earth for the final time. With Antichrist in merciless pursuit, many will be killed, and many more will flee for their lives, becoming exiled and scattered across the globe (Daniel 7:25; Zechariah 14:1–2; Matthew 24:15–21).

SECOND WORLDWIDE GATHERING IN BELIEF

5. AT THE END OF THE TRIBULATION, ISRAEL WILL BE REGATHERED IN BELIEF, IN PREPARATION FOR THE REIGN OF JESUS CHRIST ON EARTH.

As the Tribulation grinds to its final, terrible moments, Jesus Christ will return from heaven to slay the Antichrist and his armies, assembled in Israel for the final showdown. Then the Jewish people will be regathered to the land of Israel from all over the world for the second and final time, to rule and reign with their Messiah for one thousand years.

Many passages in the Bible speak of this final regathering. What a moment in history it will be! God's people will acknowledge their Messiah at His coming, the Tribulation will be over, and the door to a glorious millennial kingdom will begin to swing open. Obviously, these references are not being fulfilled by the modern state of Israel today. Some of the citations include: Deuteronomy 4:29–31; 30:1–10; Isaiah 27:12–13; 43:5–7; Jeremiah 16:14–15; 31:7–10; Ezekiel 11:14–18; Amos 9:14–15; Zechariah 10:8–12; Matthew 24:31...and many more.

God will use the unparalleled horror of the seven-year Tribulation to bring many of the Jewish people to faith in the Lord Jesus as the Messiah of God, who died for their sins and rose again on the third day (Zechariah 12:10).

We believe that this final return to the land will fulfill the Feast of Trumpets (*Rosh Hashanah*) for the nation of Israel. This regathering requires a nation made up of those who are predominately believers in Jesus as their Messiah.

The reason the Jews must accept Jesus before He can return to earth is because of their rejection of Him at His first coming. According to Matthew 23:37, Christ will return to earth only when the nation of Israel, who spurned Him at His first coming, turns to Him in repentance and faith. In Matthew 23:37–39, He declared:

> "Jerusalem, Jerusalem, who kills the prophets and stones those who are sent to her! How often I wanted to gather your children together, the way a hen gathers her chicks under her wings, and you were unwilling. Behold, you house is being left to you desolate! For I say to you, from now on you shall not see Me until you say, 'Blessed is He who comes in the name of the LORD!'"

When Christ came to earth the first time, He offered the kingdom to the Jewish people, but they were "unwilling" to receive Him. Because of the nation's rejection of Jesus as their Messiah at His first coming, Christ now pronounces judgment upon them in verse 38 and says, "Behold, your house is being left to you desolate!" What does He mean by "house"? It is a reference to the Jews' temple. Jesus continues His prophecy in verse 39: "For I say to you, from now on you shall not see Me until you say, 'Blessed is He who comes in the name of the Lord!'"

We see three key points in our Lord's statement. First, when He says, "From now on you will not see Me," Jesus speaks of His *departure*. Second, with the word *until,* he speaks of delay and postponement. Third, He looks to a time of Israel's future *repentance,* when just as they rejected Christ in the past, they will one day change their minds and realize that indeed Jesus is the nation's promised Messiah and will say, "Blessed is He who comes in the name of the Lord" (v. 39). This is the condition for the Second Coming described in the very next chapter, Matthew 24.

Arnold Fruchtenbaum further explains Matthew 23:39:

> But then He declares that they will not see Him again until they say, *Blessed is He that cometh in the name of the Lord.* This is a messianic greeting. It will mean their acceptance of the Messiahship of Jesus.
>
> So Jesus will not come back to the earth until the Jews and the Jewish leaders ask Him to come back. For just as the Jewish leaders led the nation to the rejection of the Messiahship of Jesus, they must some day lead the nation to the acceptance of the Messiahship of Jesus.[11]

Matthew 24:31 records a future regathering of Israel, this time in belief: "And He will send forth His angels with a great trumpet and they will gather together His elect from the four winds, from one end of the sky to the other." This is said to take place after the Tribulation, in conjunction with the second coming of Christ (v. 29).

Finally, all the prophecies about Israel's total possession and blessing in the land—going all the way back to God's original covenant with Abraham—will be fulfilled. And then these words of hope from the prophet Amos will come to pass: "'And they will not again be rooted out from their land which I have given them,' says the LORD your God" (9:15).

This regathering will be final.

At last.

GOD'S GRAND INDICATOR

When we think about the unprecedented worldwide regathering and reestablishment of the nation of Israel, it prompts us to look more closely at *all* the international headlines. Now that Israel is poised in the very setting required for the revealing of Antichrist and the start of the Tribulation, we begin to realize that prophetically significant events are happening all over the world.

Dr. John Walvoord says:

> Of the many peculiar phenomena which characterize the present generation, few events can claim equal significance as far as biblical prophecy is concerned with that of the return of Israel to their land. It constitutes a preparation for the end of the age, the setting for the coming of the Lord for His church, and the fulfillment of Israel's prophetic destiny.[12]

God has not—*and will not*—cast away His people. Israel is indeed God's "super sign" of the end times. She is the powder keg fuse for the final world conflict. And for the first time in almost two thousand years, the fuse is beginning to smolder.

Wonderful and terrible events lie just ahead.

WELCOME HOME

Every visitor to modern Israel who enters by plane comes in the same way. You have to go through passport control at the Ben Gurion Airport in Tel Aviv. Millions of people have come and gone through that airport, but most never even notice the big welcome sign there.

Randall Price, an expert on Israel and Bible prophecy, provides a powerful description of this welcome sign and its significance:

> Everyone arriving into Israel by plane from foreign destinations must enter the country through the Ben-Gurion Airport. Once they have passed through passport control and are about to exit, they are greeted by a huge and colorful tapestry welcoming them to the Land. On it is depicted masses of people streaming into the gates of the City of Jerusalem. On the tapestry, in Hebrew, is a prophetic text from Jeremiah that speaks about the ingathering of the exiles: "So there is hope for your future," declares the LORD. "Your children will return to their own land" (Jeremiah 3:17, NIV). Whether or not the incoming Jewish people can yet read the words, the lesson is understood, for they who are coming home are part of God's present purpose in regathering His people for the fulfillment of His promise.[13]

The number one sign of the end times is the return of the Jewish people to their homeland from worldwide exile. The coming of our Lord could be very soon.

Are you ready for the meeting in the sky?

CHAPTER FIVE

SALVATION FOR THOSE LEFT BEHIND

Soul Harvest

RAYFORD *had not been prepared for what he found on the Internet. Tsion has outdone himself. As David Hassid had said, thousands upon thousands had already responded. Many put messages on the bulletin board identifying themselves as members of the 144,000. Rayford scrolled through the messages for more than an hour, still not coming to the end. Hundreds testified that they had received Christ after reading Tsion's message and the verses from Romans that showed their need of God....*

Rayford forced himself to stay awake, poring over Tsion's teachings. A meter on his screen showed the number of responses as they were added to the central bulletin board. He believed the meter was malfunctioning. It raced so fast he could not even see the individual numerals. He sampled a few of the responses. Not only were many converted Jews claiming to be among the 144,000 witnesses, but Jews and Gentiles were also trusting Christ....

Do you see why I believe we are justified in trusting God for more than a billion souls during this period? Let us pray for that great harvest. All who name

Christ as their Redeemer can have a part in this, the greatest task ever assigned to mankind.…

Rayford could hardly keep his eyes open, but he was thrilled with Tsion's boundless enthusiasm and insightful teaching. He returned to the bulletin board and blinked. The number on the top of the screen was in the tens of thousands and rising.

SOUL HARVEST, 243, 245, 250

People who attend prophecy conferences usually bring plenty of questions to the table.

But in all the church services and conferences where we have spoken about the events of the end times, one particular question comes up more than any other. It usually goes something like this: "If a lost person hears, understands, and rejects the gospel *before* the Tribulation, will he or she be able to be saved *during* the Tribulation?"

Many people believe the answer to this question is "No!"

But in the Left Behind series, the answer is a resounding "Yes!"

Those who disagree, however, might state the issue something like this: The Left Behind view of salvation after the Rapture is a false hope and condemns people to hell by leading them to believe they will have a second chance to turn to Christ during the Tribulation.[1]

One preacher recently said that it was foolish to think that someone like Bruce Barnes (a character in Left Behind) could be an unsaved pastor before the Rapture and then find salvation *after* the Rapture. This pastor believes that Barnes, who would have heard the gospel many times prior to the Rapture, would become hardened to the message of salvation—and would no longer be capable of responding during the Tribulations days that follow. The preacher went on to warn of the danger of the Left Behind series because of this supposed error.

Since this charge against Left Behind deals with eternal salvation, it's a critically important area of discussion. But before we look at this specific issue, let's briefly consider the whole notion of salvation in the future Tribulation.

SALVATION IN A DAY OF WRATH

The events in the Left Behind series are sometimes portrayed as negative, dark, and gloomy—as bad news for planet earth.

But this depends on your perspective.

While it is true that the series depicts the horrors of the seven-year Tribulation period for those who are left behind, one of the key themes in these books is the hope found in Jesus Christ for those who turn to Him for salvation.[2] Even in the darkest hour of human history, God will still be seeking and saving that which was lost (Luke 19:10).

In Revelation 7, we are introduced to two great hosts of people who will be saved by God's grace during the Tribulation period. Here's a quick look at the contrast between these two groups.

REVELATION 7:1–8	REVELATION 7:9–17
Jews	Gentiles
144,000	no one can count
sealed	slain
on earth	in heaven

The great multitude in Revelation 7:9–17 is a host of people who are saved by God's grace during these darkest of days:

> After these things I looked, and behold, a great multitude which no one could count, from every nation and all tribes and peoples and tongues, standing before the throne and before the Lamb, clothed in white robes, and palm branches were in their hands; and they cry out with a loud voice, saying, "Salvation to our God who sits on the throne, and to the Lamb." And all the angels were standing around the throne and around the elders and the four living creatures; and they fell on their faces before the throne and worshiped God, saying, "Amen, blessing and glory and wisdom and thanksgiving and honor and power and might, be to our God forever and ever. Amen."
>
> Then one of the elders answered, saying to me, "These who are clothed in the white robes, who are they, and where have they come from?" I said to him, "My lord, you know." And he said to me, "These are the ones who come out of the great tribulation, and they have washed their robes and made them white in the blood of the Lamb. For this reason, they are before the throne of God; and they serve Him day and night in His temple; and He who sits on the throne will spread His tabernacle over them. They will hunger no longer, nor thirst anymore; nor will the sun beat down on them, nor any heat; for the Lamb in the center of the throne will be their shepherd, and will guide them to springs of the water of life; and God will wipe every tear from their eyes."

GREAT REVIVAL IN THE GREAT TRIBULATION

There have been many great spiritual revivals in history.

- The Day of Pentecost (Acts 2)
- The Reformation in Europe in the sixteenth century
- The First Great Awakening (1740s)
- The Second Great Awakening (1790s)
- The Layman's Prayer Revival (1858)

But God's Word declares that the greatest revival in human history is yet to come. The world will witness what we might call "Great Revival during the Great Tribulation."

The salvation of the lost is one of the chief purposes of the Tribulation period. The prophet Joel writes: "And anyone who calls on the name of the LORD will be saved. There will be people on Mount Zion in Jerusalem who escape, just as the LORD has said. These will be among the survivors whom the LORD has called" (2:32, NLT).

The Rapture may be the greatest evangelistic tool in human history. When millions of people disappear from the face of the earth in a split second of time, all kinds of theories and explanations will surface. But many will remember the warnings of friends and loved ones about the truth of the Rapture. In a moment of time, they will realize what has happened. They have been left behind. God will use this mind-numbing realization to bring them to faith in His Son.

Notice the picture in Revelation 7. The multitude is rejoicing greatly. Remember, these are the ones who were left behind at the Rapture—sick with apprehension, clinging to the merest thread of hope. But God reaches down and saves them out of the Tribulation.

In the midst of His wrath, God plucks them out of the fire. They will wash their robes white in the blood of the Lamb. Only a blood sacrifice of the spotless Lamb of God can cleanse us from our sins.

THE MOST IMPORTANT THOUGHT

What's the main message of Bible passages like Revelation 7? What does God want us to learn from the fact that He will save a great multitude during the Great Tribulation?

That even in judgment, God is merciful.

That even in wrath, God saves.

Think about it. Every judgment of God from the time of Noah to the judgment of His own Son on our behalf reveals the magnificent mercy of God.[3] God is in the saving, reclaiming, redemption business. He saved before the Law, and He saved under the Law. Christ will save at His Second Coming, and the door to salvation will remain open right into the millennial kingdom.

But most important for us, He saves *now*...to all who will simply call upon His name for salvation from their sins. "For whoever will call upon the name of the Lord will be saved" (Romans 10:13).

If you trust Him, He will wash away all your sins in His precious blood, just as He will do someday for those who trust Him during the Tribulation.

WHAT ABOUT THOSE WHO HAVE HEARD?

Many agree that people will find salvation after the Rapture. Scripture certainly seems clear enough about that. But what about those who heard the gospel before the Rapture, rejected it, then got left behind? Will they have another opportunity to get saved? Some strenuously object to such a notion.

Today the question we so often hear is, "What about those who *haven't* heard the Good News of Christ? Can they be saved?" During the Tribulation, the question is reversed. "What about those who *have* heard the gospel, rejected it, and missed the Rapture? Can they find salvation during the Tribulation?"

We believe that people will have the possibility to be saved in the Tribulation, regardless of how much they have been exposed to the gospel before the Rapture. Those who object to this viewpoint, however, usually refer to 2 Thessalonians 2:9–12:

> That is, the one whose coming is in accord with the activity of Satan, with all power and signs and false wonders, and with all the deception of wickedness for those who perish, because they did not receive the love of the truth so as to be saved. For this reason God will send upon them a deluding influence so that they will believe what is false, in order that they all may be judged who did not believe the truth but took pleasure in wickedness.

Proponents of this view contend that God, through the Antichrist, will actively delude those who do not believe. While this is true, nothing in the passage suggests that this delusion is a direct result of an individual's rejection of the gospel before the Rapture. What, then, is this passage really saying? Let's zoom in for a few details.

A CLOSER LOOK

In the first place, 2 Thessalonians 2 does not say anything about an individual hearing, understanding, and then rejecting the gospel. It does make a universal statement about those who do not love the truth, referring to all unbelievers in the same way. But there is no basis in this passage for identifying a subclass of unbelievers, such as those who have heard the gospel, understood it, and rejected it.

Second, the context of the entire passage relates to what will happen in the future Tribulation period. The context for "they did not receive the love of the truth" in verse 10 clearly refers to the Tribulation period itself. In other words, the passage speaks about the response of unbelievers *during* the Tribulation. If the passage were referring to an unbelieving response *prior* to the Tribulation, impacting one's destiny *during* the Tribulation, then the passage probably would have been worded differently in order to convey such a message.

But it doesn't read that way.

We see no support for the belief that a person's rejection of the gospel necessarily seals his fate if he enters the Tribulation. Specific support that verses 8–12 encompass events that will transpire in the Tribulation begins in verse 8, which says, "Then that lawless one will be revealed...." In other words, "then" denotes a shift from the current church age into a future era: the Tribulation. Nothing in 2 Thessalonians 2:8–12 takes any part of that passage out of the context of the Tribulation. Almost all would agree that 2 Thessalonians 2:8–9 refers to things the Antichrist will do during the Tribulation. Verse 10 is clearly part of that same context.

Third, the apostasy that is being spoken of in the context of 2 Thessalonians 2:3 most likely refers to events associated with the Antichrist during the middle of the Tribulation. Dr. Arnold Fruchtenbaum explains:

> These verses have often been interpreted as teaching that
> if one hears the gospel before the Rapture and rejects it,

he will not have an opportunity to be saved after the Rapture. But this is not the teaching of this passage. The point of no return is the acceptance of the "big lie" of the Antichrist's self-proclaimed deity and the submission to the worship of him by means of taking the mark of the beast. It is only then that the point of no return is actually reached. The option of taking the mark of the beast only begins in the middle of the tribulation. Even the context of this passage shows that it speaks of events that occur in the middle of the tribulation. The worshippers of the Antichrist do so because they are deceived by the Antichrist's power of miracles. They are deceived because they received not the love of the truth. The rejection of the gospel was not what they may have heard before the Rapture but rather the preaching of the 144,000 Jews and the Two Witnesses.[4]

Dr. Fruchtenbaum is correct to link this passage with events in the middle of the Tribulation. This passage lines up with events described in Revelation 12–14. The "strong delusion" of 2 Thessalonians 2:11 relates to those who receive the mark of the Beast, called "those who dwell upon the earth" throughout Revelation (3:10; 6:10; 8:13; 11:10 [twice]; 12:12; 13:8, 14 [twice]; 14:6).

We can see, then, that 2 Thessalonians 2 is a summary of Antichrist's "career" during the Tribulation period. It deals with those who reject the truth and receive the Antichrist after the Rapture. This entire passage describes events within the Tribulation period. It refers to those who witness the deception of the Antichrist, believe his message, and reject the truth. This passage says that those who do so will be condemned by God.

GOD'S SOVEREIGN GRACE

The Bible teaches that the heart of all humanity is fallen and depraved (Genesis 6:5; 8:21; Jeremiah 17:10; Ephesians 4:17–18). All unbelievers, from Adam on down, are described as being "spiritually dead" (Ephesians 2:1–3) and "blind" (2 Corinthians 4:4). For this reason, any individual believing the gospel at any time in history requires a supernatural work of the Holy Spirit. God Himself must open the sinner's eyes to the gracious offer of salvation in Christ. Left to ourselves, we will reject the gospel when it is preached. What sinner has ever heard and understood the gospel without the miraculous work of God enabling a *dead* and *blind* individual to see and believe? No sinner, on his own, has ever responded to the gospel. Unbelievers unaided by the sovereign work of God will remain in their unbelief and rejection, both during the church age and in the Tribulation to come. We believe that every unbeliever will have an opportunity to hear and believe the gospel during the Tribulation, regardless of what he heard or understood before the Rapture.

Revelation 13:8–10 says the following about the rise of Antichrist at the midpoint of the Tribulation:

> All who dwell on the earth will worship him, everyone whose name has not been written from the foundation of the world in the book of life of the Lamb who has been slain. If anyone has an ear, let him hear. If anyone is destined for captivity, to captivity he goes; if anyone kills with the sword, with the sword he must be killed. Here is the perseverance and the faith of the saints.

This speaks of destiny as the factor determining salvation: God's sovereign will! In other words, salvation during the Tribulation will come about just as it does during our present church age.

A SECOND CHANCE?

Perhaps you've heard the criticism that the Left Behind view of the end times allows a "second chance" for unbelievers who have rejected the gospel. This, too, is faulty thinking based upon a mischaracterization. The notion of a second chance, which no one will ever receive, relates to those who have departed this life through death and have gone into eternity without Christ. That is not what will be going on when any unbeliever is left behind at the Rapture. Instead, all unbelievers will simply be passing from one phase of history (the present church age) into another phase (the Tribulation). They have not left history and passed into eternity. All unbelievers passing from the church age into the Tribulation will continue to have an opportunity to receive Christ—until they have been saved, killed, or received the mark of the beast.

Undoubtedly, many who reject the gospel before the Rapture will continue to reject it after the Rapture. To claim, however, that 2 Thessalonians 2:9–12 teaches that no one who has clearly heard and rejected the claims of Christ before the Rapture can receive God's mercy during the Tribulation is just plain wrong. It is forcing the passage to say much more than the context allows. As we have seen, God will use the horror of the Tribulation period to bring millions of sinners to faith in His Son. Among this numberless crowd will certainly be some who have been given another opportunity by our gracious Lord to be saved.

EVANGELISTIC URGENCY

So why does this belief—that those who reject the gospel before the Rapture can't be saved during the Tribulation—have such a significant following?

It's no great mystery. These are sincere believers who want to drive home the urgency of receiving Jesus Christ as Savior…before it's too late. If their view is correct, then a person left behind at the Rapture would face the same fate as a person who dies without ever receiving God's offer of forgiveness in His Son. His or her doom would be sealed forever.

You can see how this would add extra urgency to the argument that unbelievers should trust Christ *now* since they may never have another opportunity. At the bottom line, however, we do not believe that this view can be supported by Scripture.

Certainly, "today is the day of salvation," and it is never advisable to delay when the Lord is calling through His gospel. The New Testament, however, teaches that an individual does not reach an unsavable position until he or she passes into eternity.

With one exception.

That exception is when the mark of the beast is issued and received during the second half of the seven-year Tribulation. Those receiving the Antichrist's mark will be finally, tragically beyond salvation (2 Thessalonians 2:9–12; Revelation 14:9–12).

When it comes to witnessing and declaring God's offer of forgiveness and salvation in Christ, we all need a sense of urgency. The time of God's grace and outstretched arms is—second by second—running out. Be that as it may, we do not need to invent devices to "help God out" with this urgency. These methods only confuse people and distort the clear message of Scripture—Jesus Christ could return at any moment, and you need to be ready by believing the gospel and serving Him.

It's easy to see why believers pleading with sinners to accept Christ would want to challenge them with all the possible ramifications of their decision. But we cannot, we must not, go beyond the limits of God's Word.

MOTIVATION ENOUGH

We believe that millions of unbelievers will be saved during the terrible time of the Tribulation. For that we can all be thankful. Many of those saved will include some who had heard the gospel many times before the Rapture. In the meantime, we believers should make every effort to preach the gospel of God's grace *before* the Rapture so that as many as possible will believe and escape the horrors of the Tribulation.

People are saved by the preaching of the gospel in the power of the Holy Spirit. As we do so, we must warn everyone we can that Jesus will come for His own at any moment of the day or night and that millions upon millions will be left behind.

That's all the motivation we need to declare the Good News…and receive it.

CHAPTER SIX

THE SEVEN-YEAR TRIBULATION

Tribulation Force

"I DON'T *know what form it will take or what the benefit will be to the Holy Land, but clearly this is the seven-year treaty.*"

Chloe looked up, "And that actually signals the beginning of the seven-year period of tribulation."

"Exactly." Bruce looked at the group. "If that announcement says anything about a promise from Carpathia that Israel will be protected over the next seven years, it officially ushers in the Tribulation."

Buck was taking notes. "So the disappearances, the Rapture, didn't start the seven-year period?"

"No," Bruce said, "Part of me hoped that something would delay the treaty with Israel. Nothing in Scripture says it has to happen right away. But once it does, the clock starts ticking."

TRIBULATION FORCE, 29

On Wednesday, April 1, A.D. 33, two days before He died on the cross for the sins of the world, Jesus gave a great sermon in which he unfolded the signs of His coming and the end of the age (Matthew 24:3).

Jesus referred to the signs of His coming as "tribulation" and compared them to a woman's labor pains (vv. 8–9). In this graphic birthing illustration, Jesus conveyed the stark truth about the end of the age. Just as birth pangs signal that a woman's time is upon her, the earth itself will suffer wave after wave of crippling pains as the Second Coming draws near. These pains will come without warning, will be irreversible, will intensify rapidly, and will get closer together. The blinding pain mounts relentlessly.

And there is no going back.

At one point in the sermon, Jesus described the hard labor that will come upon the world just before His coming: "For then there will be a great tribulation, such as has not occurred since the beginning of the world until now, nor ever will" (v. 21).

Most of the events in the Left Behind series deal with persons, places, and events that are related to the last few years of this age, a seven-year period of time most often called "the Tribulation period."

The seven-year Tribulation is a cornerstone of the entire Left Behind series. But many have questioned this notion, writing it off as just another part of the "Left Behind fiction."

Since so much of the Left Behind view of the end times deals with and relies upon the Tribulation, it's important for us to determine if this idea has any biblical support. We have to ask, "Does the Bible really teach a future seven-year time of tribulation immediately before the Second Coming of Christ? And if so, where is it taught?"

DANIEL WEIGHS IN

The truth of a worldwide time of tribulation that lasts for seven years derives primarily from the books of Daniel and Revelation.

To zero in even closer, however, we need to turn our focus to the famous "seventy weeks" prophecy in Daniel 9:24–27.

One of the most important prophetic sections in all of Scripture, this passage is the indispensable key to all prophecy. It has often been called the "backbone of Bible prophecy" and "God's prophetic time clock."

In Daniel 9:1–23, Daniel is praying, confessing his sin, and petitioning to God regarding the restoration of the Jewish people from Babylon. He knows that the seventy years of captivity is nearly over, so he begins to intercede for his people (vv. 1–2). While Daniel is still praying, God dispatches an immediate answer in the person of the angel Gabriel (v. 21).

And when that answer comes, Daniel gets far, far more than he'd bargained for. He had asked about God's plans for the next year or two. What he received was God's great plan for the ages. Daniel 9:24–27 goes far beyond the restoration of the people from Babylon—to Israel's ultimate and final restoration under Messiah.

> "A period of seventy sets of seven has been decreed for
> your people and your holy city to put down rebellion, to
> bring an end to sin, to atone for guilt, to bring in everlast-
> ing righteousness, to confirm the prophetic vision, and to
> anoint the Most Holy Place. Now listen and understand!
> Seven sets of seven plus sixty-two sets of seven will pass
> from the time the command is given to rebuild Jerusalem
> until the Anointed One comes. Jerusalem will be rebuilt
> with streets and strong defenses, despite the perilous
> times. After this period of sixty-two sets of seven, the
> Anointed One will be killed, appearing to have accom-
> plished nothing, and a ruler will arise whose armies will
> destroy the city and the Temple. The end will come with

a flood, and war and its miseries are decreed from that time to the very end. He will make a treaty with the people for a period of one set of seven, but after half this time, he will put an end to the sacrifices and offerings. Then as a climax to all his terrible deeds, he will set up a sacrilegious object that causes desecration, until the end that has been decreed is poured out on this defiler." (NLT)

As you can see, this passage is quite detailed. To help us understand it better, let's break it down into ten basic keys.

TEN KEYS TO UNDERSTANDING
THE SEVENTY WEEKS

1. IT'S ABOUT WEEKS OF YEARS

The term "week" or "sets of seven" refers to periods or sets of seven years. Daniel had already been thinking in terms of years in Daniel 9:1–2. But he had limited his focus to the seventy-year captivity of the Jewish people in Babylon.

2. THE TOTAL TIME IS 490 YEARS

The entire period involved, therefore, is a time period of 490 years (seventy sets of seven-year periods using a 360-day prophetic year).

3. IT'S ABOUT THE JEWISH PEOPLE AND THE CITY OF JERUSALEM

The 490 years concerns Daniel's people (the Jews) and the city of Jerusalem, *not* the church—"for your people and your holy city" (v. 24).

4. THE PURPOSE OF THE SEVENTY WEEKS

The purpose of these 490 years is to accomplish six divine goals. The first three have to do with man's sin, and the last three with God's righteousness (v. 24):

- "to put down rebellion"
- "to bring an end to sin"
- "to atone for guilt"
- "to bring in everlasting righteousness"
- "to confirm the prophetic vision"
- "to anoint the Most Holy Place"

Christ's death on the cross at His first coming did make provision for sin, but Israel's application of this sacrifice will not be realized until they repent at the end of the seventy weeks, in conjunction with Christ's Second Coming. The last three of these goals look ahead to the coming Kingdom Age.

5. WHEN THE CLOCK STARTED TICKING

The divine prophetic clock for the seventy weeks or 490-year period began ticking on March 5, 444 B.C., when the Persian king Artaxerxes issued a decree allowing the Jews to return under Nehemiah's leadership to rebuild the city of Jerusalem.

6. THE FIRST SIXTY-NINE WEEKS, OR 483 YEARS

From the time the countdown began until the coming of Messiah ("the Anointed One") will be 69 sets of seven (7 + 62) or 483 years. This exact period of time—173,880 days—is the precise number of days that elapsed from March 5, 444 B.C. until March 30, A.D. 33, the day that Jesus rode into Jerusalem for the Triumphal Entry

(Luke 19:27–44). The precision of this prophecy is staggering! This is a monumental proof of the inspiration of the Bible.

7. THE GAP

So far, so good. The first sixty-nine weeks have already run their course. But what about the final period of seven years or the seventieth week? When Israel rejected Jesus Christ as her Messiah, God temporarily suspended His plan for Israel. There is a gap, therefore, or parenthesis of unspecified duration, between the sixty-ninth and seventieth sets of seven.[1] Of course, Israel's rejection of her Messiah did not take God by surprise. In fact, God had already prophesied that it would happen (Deuteronomy 4:25–27).

Two specific events are prophesied in Daniel 9:26 during this gap or parenthesis:

- Messiah will be killed (this was fulfilled on April 3, A.D. 33)
- Jerusalem and the temple will be destroyed (this was fulfilled on August 6, A.D. 70).

God's prophetic clock for Israel stopped at the end of the sixty-ninth set of seven on March 30, A.D. 33. We are presently living in this period of unspecified duration between the sixty-ninth and seventieth sets of seven, called the "church age" (Ephesians 3:1–12). The church age will end when Christ comes to rapture His bride, the church, to heaven. After all, since the church wasn't around for the first sixty-nine weeks from 444 B.C. to A.D. 33, it makes sense that we won't be here for the final week of years either. *Remember, the seventy weeks have to do with Israel, not the church.* Attempting to mix these two requires excruciating mental gymnastics…and really never works.

8. ANTICHRIST'S TREATY AND THE FINAL SEVEN YEARS

God's prophetic clock for Israel will begin to run again after the church has been raptured to heaven, when the Antichrist comes onto the scene and makes a seven-year covenant with Israel (Daniel 9:27).[2] This is the final or seventieth set of seven years that still remains to be fulfilled. The covenant Antichrist will make with Israel will be a "firm," or possibly "compelled" or "forced," covenant.[3] Two events in our world today indicate that this covenant may not be far away. First, Israel was reestablished as a nation in 1948, making such a covenant possible for the first time in nineteen hundred years. Second, the current and seemingly never-ending "peace process" in the Middle East today points toward this final covenant. The stage is set for a great leader from Europe to come on the scene and give Israel a guarantee of security. As the world becomes more frustrated with the turmoil in the Middle East, this offer could very easily be a take-it-or-leave-it peace deal.

9. ANTICHRIST BREAKS THE TREATY

The Antichrist will break or terminate the covenant with Israel after three and a half years and set an abominable, sacrilegious image of himself in the rebuilt temple of God in Jerusalem (Matthew 24:15; Revelation 13:14–15). The final three and a half years will be the "great tribulation" Jesus talked about (Matthew 24:21).

10. THE END OF THE SEVENTY WEEKS

At the end of the seven years, God will slay the Antichrist at the Second Coming of Christ ("this defiler," Daniel 9:27; see 2 Thessalonians 2:8; Revelation 19:20). This will mark the end of the seventy sets of seven...and the beginning of the thousand-year reign of Christ, when the six characteristics outlined in Daniel 9:24 will be completely fulfilled (Revelation 20:1–6).

To help you better understand this incredible prophecy, here are a couple of visual aids.

OVERVIEW OF THE SEVENTY WEEKS
(DANIEL 9:24-27)

Daniel 9:24   The entire seventy weeks (490 years)

Daniel 9:25   The first sixty-nine weeks—seven weeks plus sixty-two weeks (483 years)

Daniel 9:26   The time between the sixty-ninth and seventieth weeks (indeterminate number of years, the present church age)

Daniel 9:27   The seventieth week (seven years)

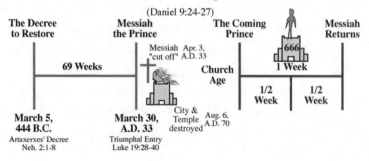

Daniel's Seventy Weeks

(Daniel 9:24-27)

DOES REVELATION TEACH A
SEVEN-YEAR TRIBULATION?

The book of Revelation never specifically mentions a seven-year period of time. That point is clear. It does, however, repeatedly mention a time of three and a half years. It is referred to variously as forty-two months (11:2; 13:5), 1,260 days (11:3; 12:6), or "a time and times and half a time" (12:14). But in every case, it equals three and a half years using the 360-day prophetic calendar.

Now where did John get the idea of a terrible time of trouble lasting three and a half years in which a great leader would rule the world? From Daniel 9:27, of course. Revelation is more dependent on Daniel than on any other Old Testament book.

You will remember that according to Daniel 9:27, the Antichrist will make a seven-year treaty with Israel. Then at the midpoint of the seven years, he will break the covenant, desecrate the temple, and launch a furious persecution of the Jewish people. The final seven-year period is divided evenly into two periods of three and a half years.

The first time a period of three and a half years is mentioned occurs in Revelation 11:2, where it's referred to as forty-two months. The next time it's mentioned is in the very next verse, where it's referred to as 1,260 days. Some scholars believe that these two periods of time refer to the two periods of three and a half years, which of course, added together equal seven years. This is one way to find a period of seven years in Revelation.

Another alternative is to take all the references to three and a half years in Revelation as relating to the last half of the seventieth week of Daniel 9:27, or the time Jesus called "great tribulation" (Matthew 24:21).

But if you adopt this view, what do you do about the first three and a half years of the Tribulation? We have to remember that the final three and a half years is not mentioned until Revelation 11:2, after the seven seal judgments and six of the trumpet judgments have been unleashed. Obviously the opening of these seals (Revelation 6) and blowing of the trumpets (Revelation 8–9) has to take some time.

John assumes his readers have a working familiarity with the Old Testament. With this in mind, he doesn't feel compelled to spell out every detail. He knows that his audience can read between the lines and fill in the gaps. The repeated mention of three and a half years in the last half of Revelation is an obvious reference back to Daniel (7:25; 9:27; 12:7). John also knows that his readers understand that the total period of time is seven years. Like Daniel, however, John focuses on the final three and a half years. But he does so assuming his readers will understand that this final three and half years is preceded by the first three and a half years.

Whichever of these views you take, John's presentation of the events of the tribulation in Revelation 6–19 is completely consistent with a seven-year period of time.

THE EARLY CHURCH AND THE FUTURE TRIBULATION

How did the early church view this future Tribulation in Scripture? It's a relevant question. Especially in light of the accusations that this teaching on a seven-year Tribulation is some recently developed interpretation.

Is it? Or has it been held by others in church history?

In fact, the early church consistently held to a gap between the sixty-ninth and seventieth weeks of Daniel. They believed in a future time of Tribulation under the reign of Antichrist. Let's consult just a couple of the more important early witnesses.

Irenaeus (A.D. 130–200), the greatest thinker in the church during the second century, taught that the Antichrist would come on the scene and rule the world for the final three and a half years before the second coming of Christ.[4] The only way he could have come to this conclusion is by seeing a gap between the sixty-ninth and seventieth weeks of Daniel 9:26–27.

Hippolytus, a disciple of Irenaeus, was bishop of Rome from A.D. 200–235. He is even clearer than his teacher about the final seven years of the end times. He wrote a commentary on Daniel that is the first known commentary on an entire book of the Bible.

In his discussion of Daniel 9:24–27, Hippolytus writes:

> For when the threescore and two weeks are fulfilled, and
> Christ is come, and the Gospel is preached in every
> place, the times being then accomplished, there will
> remain only one week, the last, in which Elijah will
> appear, and Enoch, and in the midst of it the abomina-
> tion of desolation will be manifested, viz., Antichrist,
> announcing desolation to the world.[5]

Of course, we agree that what other people believe is not the deciding issue when it comes to interpreting the Bible. The most important point about any interpretation is whether it squares with the biblical text. Nevertheless, the views of those in the early church can and should be used to corroborate what we discover in the pages of Scripture. We stand on the shoulders of those who have gone before us in the body of Christ. What is clear is that the Left Behind view of the seven-year tribulation just before the coming of Christ cannot be painted as a recent innovation. It's a legitimate, sound interpretation reflected in some of the earliest writings of the church fathers. It is a view that was held by the majority of the giants since the dawn of the church.

A GAP CALLED GRACE

The triumphal entry of Christ into Jerusalem on March 30, A.D. 33, fulfilled the most incredible prophecy ever given. Jesus appeared as Messiah the Prince exactly 173,880 days (483 years) after the decree by the Persian king Artaxerxes to restore and rebuild Jerusalem. On that day, the sixty-ninth week of Daniel's prophecy came to a close. Just four days later, however, Jesus was officially rejected by the Jewish people and crucified. Because of Israel's failure to accept Jesus as Messiah, God postponed the final seven years, or seventieth week, until the end of the age.

In the meantime, we live today in the church age—the gap of time between the end of the sixty-ninth and the beginning of the seventieth week. It has been a parenthesis in Israel's history that has extended almost two thousand years. During this time, God is calling Jews and Gentiles to faith in Jesus Christ and is making them into one body, the church.

But someday the church will be raptured to heaven, and God will directly take up His dealings with Israel once again. And since the Rapture could occur at any moment, we need to be busy doing the Lord's work. While we still have time.

Some time after the Rapture, the Antichrist will come on the scene and make a seven-year treaty, or covenant, with Israel. This event will mark the beginning of the final seven years of this world as we know it. God will use these terrible days of Tribulation to pour out His wrath on those who have rejected His Son…and pour out His grace on those who come to Him in simple faith. These final seven years will bring about the conversion of many of the Jewish people and will bring His program for them to completion.

But how much better to come to Him now, rather than then.

CHAPTER SEVEN

NEW BABYLON

Left Behind

"HE *wants to move the U.N....*"

"*Where?*"

"*He wants to move it to Babylon....*"

"*I hear they've been renovating that city for years. Millions of dollars invested in making it, what, New Babylon?*"

"*Billions....*"

"*Within a year the United Nations headquarters will move to New Babylon.*"

LEFT BEHIND, 352, 413

I n *Left Behind*, the Antichrist, Nicolae Carpathia, moves the U.N. and his world headquarters to the rebuilt city of Babylon on the Euphrates in modern Iraq, just fifty miles south of Baghdad. This breathtaking event is based on biblical prophecies found in four main places: Isaiah 13, Jeremiah 50–51, Zechariah 5:5–11, and Revelation 17–18.

Critics of the Left Behind series maintain that the prophecies of Babylon's final destruction in the Old Testament have already been fulfilled in the past. Many insist that the final reference to Babylon in Revelation 17–18 is a symbolic reference to Jerusalem or Rome, not literal Babylon.

So, is there any evidence that Babylon will be rebuilt in the end times to serve as the world headquarters of Antichrist, as depicted in the novels of Jenkins and LaHaye?

Let's take a closer look at some fascinating evidence together.

NEW BABYLON, OLD IDEA

First, let's make it clear that the Left Behind view of a rebuilt city of New Babylon in the end times is nothing new. It's been around for a long time. Many well-respected Bible teachers held and taught this view before Iraq became an independent nation in 1932—even before huge oil fields were discovered there, near Kirkuk, in 1927.

Of course, the fact that others in the past have agreed with the Left Behind view does not, by itself, prove that this interpretation is correct. But it does show that respected scholars from different vantage points, in different eras of history, working entirely on their own, have come to remarkably similar conclusions independently of one another.

Here is just a small sampling of writers from the past who taught about a literal rebuilt city of Babylon in the end times— long before the rest of us had ever heard of Saddam Hussein or the Gulf War crisis.

- J. A. Seiss—a Lutheran pastor and scholar born in 1823[1]
- Benjamin Wills Newton—originally wrote about the rebuilt city of Babylon around 1850[2]
- G. H. Pember—wrote in 1888[3]
- Clarence Larkin—wrote in 1919[4]
- Arthur W. Pink—In his excellent 1923 summary of the biblical teaching on the Antichrist, he supported the view of a rebuilt Babylon in the end times[5]

- F. E. Marsh—1925[6]
- William R. Newell—1935[7]

None of these men possibly could have dreamed that Iraq, the land of ancient Babylon, would move to the center of the world stage as it has today. Yet they believed what they saw in the Scriptures. And amazingly, what these men saw in the Word of God and accepted by faith we are now witnessing with our own eyes. These scholars didn't develop their views on Babylon by looking at the headlines. There weren't any such headlines when they wrote!

But what they believed is beginning to take shape.

We see the signs all around us. What Saddam Hussein began in rebuilding Babylon will be carried forward by others at some point. Possibly very soon and very quickly.[8]

But, of course, we can't base our view on what other people have said. So let's turn to Scripture. Let's see what we discover about Babylon and the Bible.

THE TIMING OF BABYLON'S FALL

We begin our biblical safari into the once-and-future city with the two main Old Testament passages that foretell Babylon's doom: Isaiah 13–14 and Jeremiah 50–51. In these powerful passages, God clearly announces the destruction of Babylon by a host of nations.

The *who* is clear—it's the literal city of Babylon.

The *what* is also clear—Babylon is wiped out.

But two important questions remain: *When did or when will this destruction occur?* and *Which destruction of Babylon are Isaiah and Jeremiah talking about?* Was this an event that occurred in their day? Were they prophesying about the overthrow of Babylon that occurred in 539 B.C. when the great city fell to the Medo-Persians? Or do Isaiah and Jeremiah look far, far down the road…to a future destruction of Babylon in the end times?

Join us as we consider seven important clues or pieces of evidence in Isaiah and Jeremiah that narrow down the time of Babylon's final destruction.

CLUE #1: IN THE DAY OF THE LORD

In Isaiah 13:6, 9, the Lord gives an indication of the *time* of this event. He says that the destruction will occur "in the day of the Lord":

> Wail, for the day of the LORD is near! It will come as destruction from the Almighty…. Behold, the day of the LORD is coming, cruel, with fury and burning anger, to make the land a desolation; and He will exterminate its sinners from it.

The phrase "the day of the Lord" occurs nineteen times in the Old Testament and four times in the New Testament.[9] It refers to any time that God dramatically intervenes in human affairs to bring blessing or judgment. In most cases, however, it's the latter that's in view.

The day of the Lord is when God comes down to earth to settle accounts with sinful man. There have been past, or what we might call historical, "days of the Lord" that have already occurred. For example, the destruction of Egypt by Nebuchadnezzar in 586 B.C. was called "the day of the Lord" (Ezekiel 30:3, 10). But even when a "near" day of the Lord is in view, the judgment in some way foreshadows, previews, or prefigures the final day of the Lord in the Great Tribulation (Joel 2:31; 3:14). However, the majority of references to the day of the Lord look to the final, future day of the Lord.

CLUE #2: SIGNS IN THE HEAVENS

We might agree that Babylon's destruction will occur in the day of the Lord. But *which* day of the Lord is the Bible talking about?

It's clear from the context that this destruction of Babylon will be in the *final* day of the Lord, during those horrendous years known as the Great Tribulation. Reading a little further in Isaiah 13, we are grabbed by these fearsome words:

> For the stars of heaven and their constellations will not flash forth their light; the sun will be dark when it rises and the moon will not shed its light. Thus I will punish the world for its evil and the wicked for their iniquity; I will also put an end to the arrogance of the proud and abase the haughtiness of the ruthless. I will make mortal man scarcer than pure gold and mankind than the gold of Ophir. Therefore I will make the heavens tremble, and the earth will be shaken from its place at the fury of the LORD of hosts in the day of His burning anger. (vv. 10–13)

Nothing even close to this happened in 539 B.C., when Babylon was captured by the Persians. These cosmic disturbances and supernatural signs in the heavens are described elsewhere in the Bible in conjunction with the second coming of Jesus Christ to earth.

Later in Isaiah this same language is used to describe what will happen when Jesus comes back to reign in Jerusalem: "Then the moon will be abashed and the sun ashamed, for the LORD of hosts will reign on Mount Zion and in Jerusalem, and His glory will be before His elders" (24:23).

In Joel's great prophecy of Armageddon, he mentions these same signs:

> Multitudes, multitudes in the valley of decision! For the day of the LORD is near in the valley of decision. The sun and moon grow dark and the stars lose their brightness. The Lord roars from Zion and utters His voice from Jerusalem, and the heavens and the earth tremble. But the LORD is a refuge for His people and a stronghold to the sons of Israel. (3:14–16)

In His great sermon on the end times in Matthew 24–25, Jesus actually alluded back to Isaiah 13:10, using this same kind of language to describe what will happen immediately after the Tribulation period in conjunction with His second coming.[10]

> "For just as the lightning comes from the east and flashes even to the west, so will the coming of the Son of Man be. Wherever the corpse is, there the vultures will gather. But immediately after the tribulation of those days the sun will be darkened, and the moon will not give its light, and the stars will fall from the sky, and the powers of the heavens will be shaken, and then the sign of the Son of Man will appear in the sky, and then all the tribes of the earth will mourn, and they will see the Son of Man coming on the clouds of the sky with power and great glory." (Matthew 24:27–30)

Since the destruction of Babylon is described in the same terms as Armageddon and the second coming of Christ, it will be finally destroyed at the same time.

CLUE #3: THE JUDGMENT OF THE WORLD

The time of Babylon's judgment is a time not only for that city to face judgment, but for *all* the nations to be judged. Isaiah 13:11–12 says, "Thus I will punish the world for its evil and the wicked for their iniquity; I will also put an end to the arrogance of the proud and abase the haughtiness of the ruthless. I will make mortal man scarcer than pure gold and mankind than the gold of Ophir."

When Babylon is destroyed, God will punish the world for its iniquity. And mankind will be scarcer than gold. Since this has never happened in the past, then it must refer to the future, final judgment of God at the end of the Great Tribulation.

CLUE #4: LIKE SODOM AND GOMORRAH

Isaiah 13:19 says that when Babylon is finally destroyed, it will be like Sodom and Gomorrah: "And Babylon, the beauty of kingdoms, the glory of the Chaldean's pride, will be as when God overthrew Sodom and Gomorrah."

The prophet Jeremiah says the same thing:

"Behold, she will be the least of the nations, a wilderness, a parched land and a desert. Because of the indignation of the LORD she will not be inhabited, but she will be completely desolate.... Come to her from the farthest border; open up her barns, pile her up like heaps and

utterly destroy her, let nothing be left to her.... Therefore
the desert creatures will live there along with the jackals;
the ostriches also will live in it, and it will never again be
inhabited or dwelt in from generation to generation. As
when God overthrew Sodom and Gomorrah with its
neighbors," declares the LORD, "No man will live there,
nor will any son of man reside in it." (50:12–13, 26,
39–40)

Isaiah goes on to say that Babylon will be so completely
destroyed that the city will never be dwelt in again:

It will never be inhabited or lived in from generation to
generation; nor will the Arab pitch his tent there, nor will
shepherds make their flocks lie down there. But desert
creatures will lie down there, and their houses will be full
of owls; ostriches also will live there, and shaggy goats will
frolic there. Hyenas will howl in their fortified towers and
jackals in their luxurious palaces. Her fateful time also will
soon come and her days will not be prolonged. (13:20–22)

In other words, Babylon will be totally obliterated.
Wiped off the face of the earth.
The question we are forced to ask at this point is, *When did
this ever happen in the past?* The answer is crystal clear. It didn't. It
hasn't. Nothing like this has ever happened to the city of Babylon
in its long and storied history. The city has never been destroyed
like this after Jeremiah penned his prophecy in about 600 B.C.[11]
People continued to live in the city for over a millennium after the
prophecies of Isaiah and Jeremiah. Even in modern times, Arabs
have pitched their tents in the city.

So you can see this for yourself, let's take a brief overview of Babylon's history following Judah's return from the seventy-year exile.

539 B.C.	The Persians under King Cyrus conquered Babylon in 539 B.C., but the city wasn't destroyed. The Persians simply captured the city.
450 B.C.	Herodotus, "the father of history," visited the city of Babylon. He described it in grand terms. He said the inner walls were 85 feet thick and 340 feet high with 100 gates. Obviously, at the time of his depictions, the city of Babylon—even nearly one hundred years after its fall to the Persians—was still a flourishing city of unbelievable grandeur.
332 B.C.	Alexander the Great visited the city and died there.
312 B.C.	After his death, Alexander's empire was divided among four of his generals. One of those generals, Seleucus, seized Babylon in 312.
25 B.C.	The famous geographer Strabo visited Babylon. He described the hanging garden as one of the Seven Wonders of the World. He also described the bountiful crops of barley produced in the surrounding country.
A.D. 35	On the Day of Pentecost, Jews in Jerusalem were from Babylon (Acts 2:8–10).
A.D. 64	The apostle Peter wrote his first epistle from Babylon (1 Peter 5:13).
A.D. 95	Babylon was still a viable city when the apostle John wrote the book of Revelation. He mentions it in Revelation 17–18.
A.D. 500	The Babylonian Talmud (a Jewish commentary on the Law) was promulgated from Babylon.
A.D. 917	Ibn Haukal mentions Babel as an insignificant village, but still in existence.
A.D. 1100	Babylon was again a town of some importance, being known as "The Two Mosques." Shortly afterward, it was enlarged and fortified, becoming known as Hillah ("rest"), a name it retains to this day.

So what does this tell us? It tells us that Babylon has never been destroyed as prophesied by Isaiah and Jeremiah. The city died a long, slow, agonizing death. Even today there are numerous small villages in and around the ancient city. Therefore, if the prophecies of Babylon's destruction are to be literally fulfilled (as they must be), the prophets are certainly speaking of a *future* devastation. And it is future to us as well.

Commenting on Isaiah 13:20–22, prophecy expert John Walvoord says:

> As far as the historic fulfillment is concerned, it is obvi-
> ous from both Scripture and history that these verses
> have not been literally fulfilled. The city of Babylon con-
> tinued to flourish after the Medes conquered it, and
> though its glory dwindled, especially after the control of
> the Medes and Persians ended in 323 B.C., the city con-
> tinued in some form or substance until A.D. 1000 and
> did not experience a sudden termination such as is antici-
> pated in this prophecy.[12]

CLUE #5: NO MORE BRICKS

The Bible is clear that when Babylon is destroyed, not one single stone from the city will ever be used in another building project. Jeremiah 51:26 says, "'They will not take from you even a stone for a corner nor a stone for foundations, but you will be desolate forever,' declares the LORD."

The basic problem here is that archaeological discoveries have shown that bricks and stone from ancient Babylon have been *repeatedly* plundered and reused in later construction projects. Again, the only way for this prophecy to be literally fulfilled is for

Babylon to be rebuilt and destroyed once and for all, just as the Bible predicts. When that occurs, none of the bricks from that city will ever be used again.

Clue #6: Universal rest and peace

The Bible teaches that right after Babylon's destruction, the world will enter into a time of universal rest and peace. Isaiah 14:5–8 describes the scene:

> The LORD has broken the staff of the wicked, the scepter of rulers which used to strike the peoples in fury with unceasing strokes, which subdued the nations in anger with unrestrained persecution. The whole earth is at rest and is quiet; they break forth into shouts of joy. Even the cypress trees rejoice over you, and the cedars of Lebanon, saying, "Since you were laid low, no tree cutter comes up against us."

This time of universal rest looks forward to the time of the millennial or thousand-year reign of Christ on the earth. It will come only after Babylon's utter destruction and ruin.

Clue #7: Israel's final restoration

Both Isaiah and Jeremiah predict that immediately following Babylon's destruction, Judah and Israel are restored to the land of Israel and to the Lord in an everlasting covenant. God also says that when Babylon is destroyed, the people of Israel will take their captors captive.

Right after describing Babylon's date with doom in Isaiah 13, the prophet goes on to describe what will transpire in the aftermath.

> When the LORD will have compassion on Jacob and
> again choose Israel, and settle them in their own land,
> then strangers will join them and attach themselves to
> the house of Jacob. The peoples will take them along and
> bring them to their place, and the house of Israel will
> possess them as an inheritance in the land of the LORD as
> male servants and female servants; and they will take
> their captors captive and will rule over their oppressors.
> And it will be in the day when the LORD gives you rest
> from your pain and turmoil and harsh service in which
> you have been enslaved, that you will take up this taunt
> against the King of Babylon, and say, "How the oppressor has ceased, and how fury has ceased!" (14:1–4)

Jeremiah paints the same picture.

> "Declare and proclaim among the nations. Proclaim it
> and lift up a standard. Do not conceal it but say,
> 'Babylon has been captured, Bel has been put to shame,
> Marduk has been shattered; her images have been put to
> shame, her idols have been shattered….' In those days
> and at that time," declares the LORD, "the sons of Israel
> will come, both they and the sons of Judah as well; they
> will go along weeping as they go, and it will be the LORD
> their God they will seek. They will ask for the way to
> Zion, turning their faces in its direction; they will come
> that they may join themselves to the LORD in an everlasting covenant that will not be forgotten." (50:2, 4–5)

When has this ever happened in the history of the world? When has a city called Babylon been utterly destroyed, followed by the return of the children of Israel and Judah to their ancestral homeland? When have those same returnees taken the Babylonians captive and joined in an everlasting covenant with the Lord?

We can only conclude that these events will take place at the end of the Tribulation period, when Babylon is finally eliminated and the Jewish people regather in Israel for the final time, in preparation for the thousand-year reign of Christ on earth.

THE FINAL VERDICT: BABYLON MUST BE REBUILT

We have looked at the seven pieces of evidence concerning the time of Babylon's destruction. Here they are:

1. Babylon must be destroyed in the day of the Lord.
2. Babylon's destruction will be accompanied by great signs and wonders in the heavens.
3. Babylon will be destroyed when all the world is judged.
4. Babylon will be destroyed like Sodom and Gomorrah.
5. Babylon will be destroyed so completely that not one brick will be left.
6. Babylon's destruction will usher in a time of world peace.
7. Babylon's destruction will be followed by the regathering and restoration of Israel and Judah to the land, and the Lord, in an everlasting covenant.

Now it's time for the final verdict from these Old Testament passages. We must conclude that Babylon will rise again. Since these prophecies must be literally fulfilled, they can only be fulfilled if they refer to a future city of Babylon that will be rebuilt and destroyed in the end times.

The well-known Bible teacher Clarence Larkin says:

> The destruction of Sodom and Gomorrah was not pro-tracted through many centuries, their glory disappeared in a few hours (Genesis 19:24–28), and as ancient Babylon was not thus destroyed, the prophecies of Isaiah and Jeremiah cannot be fulfilled unless there is to be a future Babylon that shall be thus destroyed.[13]

Babylon must rise again and be totally wiped out in the final day of the Lord. There's only one time in man's history when all this will occur—at the end of the Tribulation, in conjunction with the second coming of Jesus Christ.

THE LAST WORD ON BABYLON

If our conclusions from the Old Testament concerning Babylon's final destruction are correct, then we should expect to find Babylon mentioned again in the book of Revelation, which looks ahead to the climax of this age. And when we turn to that final, climactic book of Scripture, our interpretation is powerfully confirmed. In fact, it may surprise you to learn what topic or event receives the most attention in the whole book of Revelation.

You guessed it.

Babylon.

Amazingly, the book of Revelation contains 404 verses, and 42 of those verses deal with Babylon (Revelation 17–18). When you add in Revelation 14:8 and 16:19, which also speak of Babylon's future, the total number of verses dealing with Babylon goes up to

44. That's 11 percent of the entire book of Revelation devoted to one subject. Babylon.

Just think about that for a moment. It's an amazing fact. In the final book of the Bible—God's great apocalypse or "unveiling of the future"—one out of every ten verses concerns Babylon. Obviously, Babylon holds a key place in the mind of God and in His final plan for the ages.

But what does Revelation have to say about this great city?

NINE PIECES OF EVIDENCE

Babylon is mentioned in Revelation 14:8–10 and 16:18–21, but the main passage devoted to Babylon is Revelation 17–18. These chapters describe in detail the rise and fall of New Babylon.

Many scholars and Bible teachers have identified these references to Babylon as something other than the literal city of Babylon. The city of Revelation 17–18 has been variously identified as Rome, New York City, the United States, the Vatican (Roman Catholic Church), and Jerusalem,[14] just to mention a few of the main candidates.

So what's wrong with just saying that Babylon means Babylon?

We believe that the city in Revelation 17–18 refers to a literal rebuilt city of Babylon in modern-day Iraq on the Euphrates River, which God will destroy at the end of the Tribulation. Nine main points favor this identification.

1. "BABYLON" MEANS BABYLON

First, Revelation is filled with the names of many geographical places: Ephesus, Smyrna, Pergamum, Thyatira, Sardis, Philadelphia, Laodicea, Patmos. These names are almost universally understood as the literal locations mentioned. Even Armageddon, in Revelation 16:16, is a literal piece of real estate in northern Israel.

The one time John wants to identify a location using symbolic language, he alerts the reader to the fact that it is nonliteral. In Revelation 11:8 he refers to Jerusalem as "the great city which mystically is called Sodom and Egypt."

John makes it clear he is *not* being literal. Jerusalem is "mystically" called Sodom and Egypt. The fact that John is careful to let the reader know when he is not speaking literally of a geographical location leads us to believe that when he leaves that part out, he intends for us to take it at face value.

In Revelation, the great city is specifically called Babylon six times (14:8; 16:19; 17:5; 18:2, 10, 21). While it is possible that the name Babylon is code for Rome, New York, Jerusalem, or some other city, getting to that point of view requires some difficult mental and exegetical gymnastics! Since the text offers no indication that it is to be taken figuratively or symbolically, it makes a great deal more sense to take it as referring to literal Babylon.

Henry Morris supports this literal understanding of Babylon. "It must be stressed again," he writes, "that *Revelation* means 'unveiling,' not 'veiling.' In the absence of any statement in the context to the contrary, therefore, we must assume that the term Babylon applies to the real city of Babylon, although it also may extend far beyond that to the whole system centered at Babylon as well."[15]

2. In the wilderness

In Revelation 17:3 we read that the woman, identified as Babylon, was out in the wilderness: "And he carried me away in the Spirit into a wilderness; and I saw a woman sitting on a scarlet beast."

The mention of the wilderness is probably an allusion to the "oracle concerning the wilderness of the sea" in Isaiah 21:1, which includes the statement "fallen, fallen is Babylon" (v. 9). The wilderness of the sea is the sandy wastes or sea country in the Persian Gulf area outside of Babylon on the Euphrates.

This is a clear link between Babylon in Revelation 17 and the literal city of Babylon in the Old Testament.

3. Daniel continued

Although Daniel is not the most frequently quoted Old Testament book in Revelation, we believe it is the one that most influenced the apostle John. Revelation 4–22 is almost a continuation of Daniel. It's like the sequel—in a sense it could be called "Daniel, part two." So let's check it out: When Daniel mentions Babylon, what does he mean?

Literal Babylon, of course.

If Daniel is the key background book for Revelation, then what should we assume *Babylon* means in Revelation unless told otherwise? It has to mean *literal Babylon*.

4. The tale of two cities

From the very beginning in the Bible, Babylon is presented as man's city—man built it to make a name for himself. But to an even greater extent it was also *Satan's* city. He was the power behind almost everything that went on there. Babylon was the first city built after the flood. It was the place man first gathered in collective rebellion against God. Indeed, Babylon literally means "city of confusion."

After the tenth and eleventh chapters of Genesis, Babylon is next mentioned in Genesis 14, where Chedorlaomer, the king of Shinar (Babylon), leads an invading force of five armies into the land of Canaan. This is the first war recorded in the Bible. And who leads it? The King of Babylon. Now, in addition to its notoriety as the original place of rebellion, pride, and false religion, Babylon also plays a major role in the first war!

In contrast to Babylon, Jerusalem is pictured as God's city. Jerusalem is also mentioned for the first time in Genesis 14. Called Salem at that time, it's the city in which the mysterious figure named Melchizedek lived. After Abraham defeated Chedorlaomer, Melchizedek came out from Salem to meet him as he returned, bringing bread and wine. Interestingly, Melchizedek was "a priest of God Most High" (v. 18); his name means "king of righteousness." Salem means "city of peace." Melchizedek was a king-priest of Salem/Jerusalem who prefigured the ultimate king-priest of Jerusalem, Jesus Christ (Psalm 110:4–7; Hebrews 7:1–28).

About one thousand years later, God chose Jerusalem for King David to establish as his capital city. And later, under Solomon, it became the place to which God chose to come and dwell on earth in the Holy of Holies of the temple. In a very literal sense, Jerusalem is God's city on earth.

While Jerusalem and Babylon first appear together in Genesis 14, the last time they appear together is in Revelation 17–18 (for Babylon) and Revelation 21:1–22:5 (for the New Jerusalem). Henry Morris, in his excellent commentary on Revelation, says, "The harlot Babylon is a contrasting type of the chaste Jerusalem and, in one sense, the whole course of history is essentially a tale of these two great spiritual cities."[16]

Compare what the Bible tells us about Jerusalem, God's own city, to what it tells us about Babylon:

JERUSALEM-BABYLON COMPARISONS	
JERUSALEM	**BABYLON**
Most mentioned city in the Bible	Second most mentioned city
City of peace	City of confusion and war
God's temple was there	Man's tower was there
Chaste Bride (Revelation 21:9)	**Great Harlot** (Revelation 17:1)
River of God (Revelation 22:1)	**River Euphrates**
"Then one of the seven angels who had the seven bowls full of the seven last plagues came and spoke with me, saying, 'Come here, I shall show you the bride, the wife of the Lamb.'" (Revelation 21:9)	"Then one of the seven angels who had the seven bowls came and spoke with me, saying, 'Come here, I shall show you the judgment of the great harlot who sits on many waters.'" (Revelation 17:1)
"And he carried me away in the Spirit to a great high mountain, and showed me the holy city, Jerusalem, coming down out of heaven from God." (Revelation 21:10).	"And he carried me away in the Spirit into a wilderness; and I saw a woman sitting on a scarlet beast, full of blasphemous names, having seven heads and ten horns." (Revelation 17:3).
Eternal, from God (Revelation 21:2)	**Destroyed by God** (Revelation 18:8)
God's city (Revelation 21:2)	**Satan's city** (Revelation 18:2)

The Bible ends as it begins…with man gathered in rebellion against God at Babylon in Revelation 17–18. But all who humbly submit to God by putting their trust in Him have their part in the New Jerusalem, the city of eternal peace and rest.

5. LOCATION, LOCATION, LOCATION

The city of Babylon on the Euphrates fits the criteria for this city as described in Revelation 17–18. Henry Morris highlights the advantages of Babylon as a world capital.

> Nevertheless, Babylon is indeed a prime prospect for rebuilding, entirely apart from any prophetic intimations. Its location is the most ideal in the world for any kind of international center. Not only is it in the beautiful and fertile Tigris-Euphrates plain, but it is near some of the world's richest oil reserves.
>
> Computer studies for the Institute of Creation Research have shown, for example, that Babylon is very near the geographical center of all the earth's land masses. It is within navigable distances to the Persian Gulf and is at the crossroads of the three great continents of Europe, Asia, and Africa.
>
> Thus there is no more ideal location anywhere for a world trade center, a world communications center, a world banking center, a world educational center, or especially, a world capital! The greatest historian of modern times, Arnold Toynbee, used to stress to all his readers and hearers that Babylon would be the best place in the world to build a future world cultural metropolis.
>
> With all these advantages, and with the head start already made by the Iraqis, it is not far-fetched at all to suggest that the future capital of the "United Nations Kingdom," the ten-nation federation established at the beginning of the tribulation should be established there.[17]

6. THE RIVER EUPHRATES

The Euphrates River is mentioned by name twice in Revelation (9:14; 16:12). In Revelation 9:14, the text states that four fallen angels are being held at the Euphrates River awaiting the appointed time for them to lead forth a host of demons to destroy one-third of mankind. In Revelation 16:12, the sixth bowl judgment is poured out and dries up the Euphrates River to prepare the way for the kings of the east. These references to the Euphrates point to the fact that something important and evil is occurring there. The rebuilt city of Babylon on the Euphrates functioning as a great commercial and political center for Antichrist is a good explanation for this emphasis on the Euphrates River in Revelation.

7. TWO EVIL WOMEN

Zechariah 5:5–11 records an incredible vision that pertains to the city of Babylon in the end times:

> Then the angel who was talking with me came forward and said, "Look up! Something is appearing in the sky." "What is it?" I asked. He replied, "It is a basket for measuring grain, and it is filled with the sins of everyone throughout the land." When the heavy lead cover was lifted off the basket, there was a woman sitting inside it. The angel said, "The woman's name is Wickedness," and he pushed her back into the basket and closed the heavy lid again. Then I looked up and saw two women flying toward us, with wings gliding on the wind. Their wings were like those of a stork, and they picked up the basket

and flew with it into the sky. "Where are they taking the basket?" I asked the angel. He replied, "To the land of Babylonia, where they will build a temple for the basket. And when the temple is ready, they will set the basket there on its pedestal." (NLT)

The prophet, writing in about 520 B.C., twenty years after the fall of Babylon to the Medo-Persians, saw evil returning to its original place in the future—the land of Babylon.

The parallels between Zechariah 5:5–11 and Revelation 17–18 are striking.

ZECHARIAH 5:5–11	REVELATION 17–18
woman sitting in a basket	woman sitting on the beast, seven mountains and many waters (17:3, 9, 15)
emphasis on commerce (a basket for measuring grain)	emphasis on commerce (merchant of grain [18:13])
woman's name is Wickedness	woman's name is "Babylon the Great, Mother of all Prostitutes and Obscenities in the World" (17:5, NLT)
focus on false worship (a temple is built for the woman)	focus on false worship (18:1–3)
woman is taken to Babylon	woman is called Babylon

God's Word teaches that in the end times, wickedness will again rear its ugly head in the same place where it began—

Babylon. The prostitute of John's account will fulfill Zechariah 5:5–11, as Babylon is established in the last days as the economic world capital embodying every kind of evil.

Revelation 18:10–18 lists the twenty-nine things that Babylon trades as the center of world commerce.

> "'Woe, woe, the great city, Babylon, the strong city! For in one hour your judgment has come.'
>
> "And the merchants of the earth weep and mourn over her, because no one buys their cargoes any more— cargoes of gold and silver and precious stones and pearls and fine linen and purple and silk and scarlet, and every kind of citron wood and every article of ivory and every article made from very costly wood and bronze and iron and marble, and cinnamon and spice and incense and perfume and frankincense and wine and olive oil and fine flour and wheat and cattle and sheep, and cargoes of horses and chariots and slaves and human lives. The fruit you long for has gone from you, and all things that were luxurious and splendid have passed away from you and men will no longer find them. The merchants of these things, who became rich from her, will stand at a distance because of the fear of her torment, weeping and mourning, saying, 'Woe, woe, the great city, she who was clothed in fine linen and purple and scarlet, and adorned with gold and precious stones and pearls; for in one hour such great wealth has been laid waste!' And every shipmaster and every passenger and sailor, and as many as make their living by the sea, stood at a distance, and were crying out as they saw the smoke of her burning, saying, 'What city is like the great city?'"

Babylon is clearly portrayed as the commercial center of the world.

8. THE DESTRUCTION OF BABYLON

As we have already carefully noted, the city of Babylon was never destroyed suddenly and completely as is predicted in Isaiah 13–14 and Jeremiah 50–51. The statements concerning Babylon's destruction in Revelation 17–18 are conspicuously similar to the description of her doom in these Old Testament passages. This leads us to believe that the same city is in view in all of these passages.

9. BABYLON IN PAIRS

Jeremiah 50–51 is a pair of chapters that serve as a kind of Old Testament counterpart to Revelation 17–18. The Jeremiah passage clearly describes the geographical city of Babylon on the Euphrates. The many parallels between this description and the future Babylon in Revelation 17–18 indicate that they are both describing the same city.

PARALLELS BETWEEN JEREMIAH 50–51 AND REVELATION 17–18[18]		
	Jeremiah 50–51	**Revelation 17–18**
compared to a golden cup	51:7a	17:3–4 and 18:6
dwelling on many waters	51:13a	17:1
involved with nations	51:7b	17:2
named the same	50:1	18:10
destroyed suddenly	51:8a	18:8

	Jeremiah 50–51	Revelation 17–18
destroyed by fire	51:30b	17:16
never to be inhabited	50:39	18:21
punished according to her works	50:29	18:6
fall illustrated	51:63–64	18:21
God's people flee	51:6, 45	18:4
heaven to rejoice	51:48	18:20

PARALLELS BETWEEN JEREMIAH 50–51 AND REVELATION 17–18[18]

Someone has said that the book of Revelation is the Grand Central Station of the Bible, because it's where all the trains of thought in the whole Bible come in. That's exactly what we have seen. In Revelation 17–18, Babylon's train comes in.

And it might not be very far down the tracks at this very moment.

FUTURE TENSE

The city of New Babylon will be rebuilt in Iraq in the last days as a great world political and economic center for Antichrist's empire.

The rise of Iraq on the world political and economic scene in recent years is no accident. Neither are her huge reserves of oil and their resulting revenues.

God put that oil there. It's one of the means God is using to draw world attention back to the Middle East as the sands of time are running out. In spite of two Gulf wars and tremendous world-wide pressure, Iraq remains a nation that occupies a prime piece of real estate. The rebuilding of Babylon begun by Saddam Hussein and the rise of Iraq on the world scene point toward the ancient prophecies of Babylon's role in the end times.

Keep one eye toward the sky. Jesus may come very soon.

CHAPTER EIGHT

ANTICHRIST

Nicolae

———

BRUCE *spent the next several hours giving Buck a crash course in prophecy and the end times. Buck had heard much of the information about the Rapture and the two witnesses, and he picked up snippets about the Antichrist. But when Bruce got to the parts about the great one-world religion that would spring up, the lying, so-called peacemaker who would bring bloodshed through war, the Antichrist who would divide the world into ten kingdoms, Buck's blood ran cold. He fell silent, no longer peppering Bruce with questions or comments. He scribbled notes as fast as he could.*

Did he dare tell this unpretentious man that he believed Nicolae Carpathia could be the very man the Scriptures talked about? Could all this be coincidental? His fingers began to shake when Bruce told of the prediction of a seven-year pact between Antichrist and Israel, of the rebuilding of the temple, and even of Babylon becoming headquarters for a new world order.

LEFT BEHIND, 425–426

One of the principal characters in Left Behind's presentation of the end time drama is a shrewd, vicious world ruler.

The Antichrist.

In the fiction of LaHaye and Jenkins, the Antichrist is a Romanian born leader who catapults from within the reunited Roman empire in Europe to center stage, on a platform of world peace mixed with his mesmerizing charisma and charm. The Antichrist makes a seven-year peace treaty with Israel and appears to be the long awaited Messiah of the world.

But then the mask comes off.

At the midpoint of the seven-year treaty, he breaks his covenant with Israel. Beginning a three-and-a-half year reign of terror, he mercilessly persecutes the Jewish people and those who have accepted Christ after the Rapture. He demands worship from the whole world and even imposes his own unique mark on the population of earth as a prerequisite to engage in commerce.

Antichrist rules the entire world politically, economically, and religiously for the final three and a half years of this age.

This view of the Antichrist is derived from many biblical passages, including Daniel 7–11; Matthew 24:23–24; 2 Thessalonians 2:3–8; Revelation 13:1–18; and 17:9–17. The only places in the New Testament where the term *Antichrist* actually appears, however, are in 1 John 2:18, 22; 4:3, and 2 John 1:7.

One of the consistent criticisms of Left Behind is its presentation of a future, individual, personal Antichrist. So let's examine those critiques and see how they stand up to careful scrutiny.

THE STRAW MAN

Gary DeMar attacks the Left Behind view of the Antichrist on three major grounds. First, he points out how many people throughout history have tried and failed to guess the identity of the Antichrist.[1] Of course, DeMar is correct on this point, but it has nothing to do with the real issue of whether there will be a personal Antichrist in the end times. Just because some people have engaged in unbiblical speculation that turned out to be false, does not mean that the entire idea of a personal Antichrist is false. This straw man argument really proves nothing.[2]

In fact, the authors of the Left Behind series—and the authors of this book as well—have never engaged in this kind of "Antichrist name game." All four of us would say, rather emphatically, that *no one* can determine the identity of the Antichrist until after the Rapture. And this is the view that is clearly presented in Left Behind. The identity of the Antichrist is not discovered until after the church of Jesus Christ has been instantly translated into His presence. We believe this to be the biblical position, as presented in 2 Thessalonians 2:1–3.

DeMar's first argument, then, is really a kind of smoke screen. The authors of Left Behind have neither promoted nor participated in a fruitless name-the-Antichrist guessing game.

aNTICHRISTS AND ANTICHRIST

Gary DeMar's second attack centers on the New Testament books of 1 and 2 John. Starting with these passages, he seeks to make his case against a future, personal Antichrist—since these are the only places the actual term appears. The word *Antichrist* (*antichristos*) is found only five times in the New Testament, all in the letters of John (1 John 2:18, 22; 4:3; 2 John 1:7).

Children, it is the last hour; and just as you have heard
that antichrist is coming, even now many antichrists
have appeared; from this we know that it is the last hour.
(1 John 2:18)

Who is the liar but the one who denies that Jesus is the
Christ? This is the antichrist, the one who denies the
Father and the Son. (1 John 2:22)

And every spirit that does not confess Jesus is not from
God; this is the spirit of the antichrist, of which you have
heard that it is coming, and now it is already in the
world. (1 John 4:3)

For many deceivers have gone out into the world, those
who do not acknowledge Jesus Christ as coming in the
flesh. This is the deceiver and the antichrist. (2 John 1:7)

Commenting on these verses, DeMar is dogmatic about their
meaning. He writes:

Yet one cannot reach this conclusion by studying John's
biblical description of Antichrist.[3]

Not one of John's statements relates to the modern doctrine of the Antichrist as outlined by LaHaye and many
other prophecy writers.[4]

According to the Bible, Antichrist is not a single individual.[5]

We take strong issue with these statements. We further believe
that they are contrary to what the apostle John is actually teaching.

In his three New Testament letters, the beloved disciple primarily concerns himself with the doctrinal error of denying the person of Jesus Christ. John states that even in his own day many "antichrists" (false teachers) had arisen who were denying the true Christ and deceiving many. The emphasis in John's letters is on the immediate doctrinal error of his own day. The antichrists in John's day, however, were only the initial stage of the antichrist philosophy that Satan had already set into motion (1 John 4:3; 2 Thessalonians 2:7).

Notice in 1 John 2:18 that John refers to antichrist (*antichristos*, singular) who is coming in the future and antichrists (*antichristoi*, plural) who are already present.[6] John's use of the singular for the Antichrist—in stark contrast to the plural antichrists—clearly denotes a single individual. By using both the singular and the plural, John teaches that the contemporary antichrists in his day, who were the false teachers, embodied the denying, deceiving spirit of the future Antichrist. They were forerunners of the final Antichrist, and powerful evidence that his spirit was already at work in the world.

Interestingly, this is the overwhelming view of evangelical scholars. Every well-known, respected New Testament scholar we could find disagrees with DeMar's interpretation of "antichrist" in 1 John.[7]

James Montgomery Boice is representative of this almost universal view. "He is saying that the spirit that will characterize the final antichrist is already working in those who have recently left his readers' congregations. The future antichrist will be a substitute for Christ, as much like Jesus as possible for a tool of Satan to be."[8]

Renowned scholar F. F. Bruce agrees: "So it was with John. That Antichrist would come he and his readers knew, and in the false teachers he discerned the agents, or at least the forerunners, of Antichrist, sharing his nature so completely that they could be called 'many antichrists.'"[9]

In other words, John looks beyond his own day and the many antichrists (lowercase *a*), to the one ultimate Antichrist (capital *A*) who will culminate the manifestation of the lawless system that denies Christ and deceives men.

ANTICHRIST IS COMING!

First John 2:18 says, "Children, it is the last hour; and just as you have heard that antichrist is coming, even now many antichrists have appeared; from this we know that it is the last hour." John's readers knew about the predicted advent of the future, final Antichrist. They had heard that Antichrist was coming. The title "Antichrist" might have been new, but the idea was not.

When and where had John's readers heard about this? The answer is really quite simple. John had undoubtedly personally taught them about the Antichrist—and they had certainly read about his coming in Old Testament books such as Daniel. Years earlier, when Paul was in Ephesus, he had also taught these same believers what John was now addressing in his letters. These Christians had clearly heard about the coming of this final great deceiver, just as Paul had taught the Thessalonian believers (2 Thessalonians 2:1–12).[10]

John's purpose was to warn his fellow believers about present false teachers who came in the spirit of Antichrist, displaying rabid hostility toward the true and living Christ.

ANTI CHRIST

Before we go any further in this discussion of Antichrist, it's important that we pull over and park—just briefly—to make sure we know who we are really talking about.

The prefix *anti* can mean "against"/"opposed to" or "instead of"/"in place of." So what does *anti* mean when we speak of Antichrist? Does it mean *against* Christ or *in place of* Christ? In other words, are we talking about opposition here or a substitution? Will he be a false, counterfeit Messiah or simply work against Christ Himself?

Both of these meanings are undoubtedly included in the term *Anti*christ. He will be the archenemy and the ultimate opponent of the Lord Jesus. The origin, nature, and purpose of Christ and Antichrist are diametrically opposed. The following list reveals the gaping chasm between Christ and His adversary.[11]

CHRIST	ANTICHRIST
The Truth	The Lie
The Holy One	The Lawless One
The Man of Sorrows	The Man of Sin
The Son of God	The Son of Destruction
The Mystery of Godliness	The Mystery of Iniquity
Cleanses the Temple	Desecrates the Temple
The Lamb	The Beast

The total opposition of Antichrist to Christ is seen in these contrasting descriptions.[12]

FEATURE	CHRIST	ANTICHRIST
Origin:	Heaven	Bottomless pit
Nature:	The Good Shepherd	The foolish shepherd
Destiny:	To be exalted on high	To be cast down into hell
Goal:	To do His Father's will	To do his own will
Purpose:	To save the lost	To destroy the holy people
Authority:	His Father's Name	His own name
Attitude:	Humbled Himself	Exalts himself
Fruit:	The True Vine	The vine of the earth
Response:	Despised	Admired

In every area that can be imagined, Christ and Antichrist are fundamentally opposed.

The Antichrist will not only be "anti" Christ, in the sense of being against Him, but he will also be "anti" Christ in the sense of "in place of" Christ. He will be an amazing parody or counterfeit of the true Christ. He will be a substitute Christ, a mock Christ, a pseudo Christ, an imitation Christ.

In John 5:43, Jesus said, "I have come in My Father's name, and you do not receive Me; if another comes in his own name, you will receive him." The one coming in his own name will be the world's final false Messiah, the Antichrist. He will attempt to be the "alter ego" of the true Christ.

Satan has never originated anything except sin. He has always counterfeited the works of God. Antichrist is no exception. He is Satan's ultimate masterpiece—a false Christ and forged replica of Jesus, the true Christ and Son of God.

Here are twenty ways Antichrist will mimic the ministry of the true Son of God.

CHRIST	ANTICHRIST
Miracles, signs, wonders (Matthew 9:32–33; Mark 6:2)	Miracles, signs, wonders (Matthew 24:24; 2 Thessalonians 2:9)
Appears in the millennial temple (Ezekiel 43:6–7)	Sits in the Tribulation temple (2 Thessalonians 2:4)
Is God (John 1:1–2; 10:35–36)	Claims to be God (2 Thessalonians 2:4)
Is the Lion from Judah (Revelation 5:5)	Has a mouth like a lion (Revelation 13:2)
Makes a peace covenant with Israel (Ezekiel 37:26)	Makes a peace covenant with Israel (Daniel 9:27)
Causes men to worship God (Revelation 1:6)	Causes men to worship Satan (Revelation 13:3–4)
Followers sealed on their forehead (Revelation 7:4; 14:1)	Followers sealed on their forehead or right hand (Revelation 13:16–18)
Worthy name (Revelation 19:16)	Blasphemous names (Revelation 13:1)
Married to a virtuous bride (Revelation 19:7–10)	Married to a vile prostitute (Revelation 17:3–5)
Crowned with many crowns (Revelation 19:12)	Crowned with ten crowns (Revelation 13:1)
Is the King of kings (Revelation 19:16)	Is called "the king" (Daniel 11:36)
Sits on a throne (Revelation 3:21; 12:5; 20:11)	Sits on a throne (Revelation 13:2; 16:10)
Sharp sword from his mouth (Revelation 19:15)	Bow in his hand (Revelation 6:2)
Rides a white horse (Revelation 19:11)	Rides a white horse (Revelation 6:2)
Has an army (Revelation 19:14)	Has an army (Revelation 6:2; 19:19)
Violent death (Revelation 5:6; 13:8)	Violent death (Revelation 13:3)
Resurrection (Matthew 28:6)	Resurrection (Revelation 13:3, 14)
Second Coming (Revelation 19:11–21)	Second Coming (Revelation 17:8)
Thousand-year worldwide kingdom (Revelation 20:1–6)	Three-and-a-half-year worldwide kingdom (Revelation 13:5–8)
Part of a Holy Trinity (Father, Son and Holy Spirit) (2 Corinthians 13:14)	Part of an unholy trinity (Satan, Antichrist and False Prophet) (Revelation 13)

J. Dwight Pentecost aptly summarizes the meaning of the word Antichrist. "Satan is seeking to give the world a ruler in place of Christ who will also be in opposition to Christ so that he can rule over the world, instead of Christ."[13]

AKA (ALSO KNOWN AS)

Without any doubt, the most familiar and commonly used title in Christianity for the sinister end-time world ruler is Antichrist. But this is not his only designation in the Bible. It shouldn't surprise us to see Antichrist referred to by various names and titles. Just as Christ is known by different names and titles throughout the Scripture, the one who will come to imitate and oppose Him is also known by various designations.

A. W. Pink, the great theologian, notes, "Across the varied scenes depicted by prophecy there falls the shadow of a figure at once commanding and ominous. Under many different names, like the aliases of a criminal, his character and movements are set before us."[14]

Here are the top ten aliases for the coming Antichrist predicted in the Bible.[15]

1. the little horn (Daniel 7:8)
2. a king, insolent and skilled in intrigue (Daniel 8:23)
3. the prince who is to come (Daniel 9:26)
4. the one who makes desolate (Daniel 9:27)
5. the king who does as he pleases (Daniel 11:36)
6. a foolish shepherd (Zechariah 11:15)
7. the man of lawlessness (2 Thessalonians 2:3)
8. the son of destruction (2 Thessalonians 2:3)
9. the rider on the white horse (Revelation 6:2)
10. the Beast out of the Sea (Revelation 13:1–9; 17:3, 8)

THE EARLY CHURCH AND THE
END TIME ANTICHRIST

DeMar's third main criticism of the Left Behind view of Antichrist is that it is a "modern" formulation. A contemporary myth. He repeatedly refers to the Left Behind view of the Antichrist as "the modern Antichrist doctrine," "LaHaye's modern Antichrist doctrine," and "the modern doctrine of the Antichrist as outlined by LaHaye and many other prophecy writers."[16]

But is the Left Behind view of the Antichrist a myth? Is it even modern? The evidence reveals that this teaching goes all the way back to the earliest days of the church. Here is a brief outline of what the early church believed about the Antichrist.

The *Didache,* or Teaching of the Twelve Apostles, was written sometime between A.D. 70–100. This early church document recognized the future coming of a personal Antichrist who would bring a time of unparalleled trouble on the earth.

> For as lawlessness increases, they will hate and perse-
> cute and betray one another. And then the deceiver of
> the world will appear as a son of God and "will per-
> form signs and wonders," and the earth will be
> delivered into his hands, and he will commit abomina-
> tions the likes of which have never happened
> before."[17]

Irenaeus was the premier Christian thinker of the second century A.D. He included a treatment on the Antichrist in his great work *Against Heresies.* In that work he detailed his view of the coming evil one.

Antichrist is a single individual whose coming was still future in the second century A.D. He will totally embody evil just as Christ does good.[18]

Antichrist will be a Jew from the tribe of Dan.[19]

Antichrist will reign over the world for a period of three and a half years.[20]

Hippolytus was presbyter of Rome from about A.D. 200–235. He wrote the first surviving, complete Christian biblical commentary titled *Commentary on Daniel.* Writing in about A.D. 204, Hippolytus also penned an entire treatise concerning Antichrist called *On the Antichrist.* This early church father listed six ways in which Antichrist will be a perverted imitation of Christ:

1) Jewish origin; 2) the sending out of apostles; 3) bringing together people spread abroad; 4) sealing of his followers; 5) appearance in the form of a man; and 6) the building of a temple in Jerusalem.[21]

He also taught that Antichrist would rise from a ten-kingdom form of the Roman empire, that he would rebuild the Roman empire, that his career would last for three and a half years, and that he would persecute Christians who would not worship him.[22]

Tertullian was the first major voice in Latin Christianity, who lived from about A.D. 160–220.

ANTICHRIST 139

Tertullian makes it clear that he believed both in present "antichrists," who were heretics who divided the church, and also in a coming final Antichrist who will persecute God's people.[23]

Cyril, bishop of Jerusalem, lived from about A.D. 315–386.

Based on Daniel 7:13–27, 2 Thessalonians 2:4, and other passages commonly related to Antichrist, Cyril expected a single Antichrist who will be a powerful, skilled worker of magic and sorcery. He will be the eleventh king of the fragmented Roman empire and will rebuild the destroyed Jewish temple and enthrone himself there as god.[24]

Jerome (331–420), the great Latin father of the church, also believed in a personal Antichrist.

Jerome too believed Antichrist would be a Jew, but he also held that he would be born of a virgin and indwelt by Satan himself. He also taught that the Roman empire would be partitioned by ten kings who would be overcome by Antichrist, the eleventh king. He also believed Antichrist would die on the Mount of Olives, the same place where Christ ascended to heaven.[25]

Bernard McGinn, a noted expert on the Antichrist, quotes David Dunbar, a renowned patristic scholar, who says that a "kind of mainline eschatology" had developed that was

quite widespread during the closing decades of the second century. This mainline view in the church was that

Antichrist would be a future Jewish individual from the tribe of Dan; he will come after the fragmentation of the Roman empire; he will be a persecuting tyrant; he will rebuild the temple in Jerusalem; he will exalt himself as god; he will rule for three and a half years; his fall will usher in Christ's return to earth.[26]

As you can see, this view of the Antichrist from the earliest days of church history strikingly resembles the Left Behind view of Antichrist. In fact, the Left Behind picture of this coming world leader is almost a mirror image of the early church fathers' view.

Far from being modern, the Left Behind view of Antichrist is actually the ancient and historical view of the church.

WAITING IN THE WINGS

By carefully examining Scripture, we discover that the Left Behind view of a personal, individual, future Antichrist isn't unbiblical at all. In fact, it's the view that lines up best with all the relevant passages.

On top of that, this view is validated when we take a look at church history. The Left Behind presentation of a personal Antichrist is the overwhelming view of the early church, and of the most respected, competent evangelical scholars in the last century.

While people can and do legitimately disagree over particular details of the Antichrist's character and career, the Bible is clear that he will make his entrance on the world stage in the end times.

Make no mistake about it. Antichrist is coming!

And it could be very soon.

CHAPTER NINE

THE MARK OF THE BEAST

The Mark

"MANY *of you know that Ms. Ivins helped raise me. Indeed for many years I believed she was my aunt—we were that close. She has been working on a project that will help me put in place certain unfortunately necessary controls on the citizenry. Most people are devoted to me—we know that. Many who were not or who were undecided are not decidedly with us, and, you will agree for good reason.*

"But there are those factions, primarily the two that I have already mentioned, who are not loyal. Perhaps now they have seen the error of their ways and will henceforth be loyal. If so, they will have no trouble with the safeguards I feel must be initiated. I am asking those loyal to the Global Community, specifically to me and to the unified faith, to willingly bear a mark of loyalty...."

"Every man, woman, and child, regardless of their station in life, shall receive this mark on their right hands or on their foreheads. Those who neglect to get the mark when it is made available will not be allowed to buy or sell until such time as they receive it. Those who overtly

refuse shall be put to death, and every marked loyal citi-
zen shall be deputized with the right and responsibility to
report such a one. The mark shall consist of the name of
His Excellency or the prescribed number."

THE MARK, 83–85

T he mark of the beast has been the focal point of more rheto-
ric, ridicule, argumentation, and speculation than any other
single item in Bible prophecy—and possibly in the entire
Bible. Christians and non-Christians have argued with each other,
and believers have sharply disagreed even among themselves. Our
friend Dr. Harold Willmington has rightly said, "There's been a lot
of sick, sick, sick about six, six, six."

Understandably, one entire book in the Left Behind series is
devoted to the mark of the beast, or 666. In *The Mark,* the
Antichrist, Nicolae Carpathia, requires everyone in the world to
take his mark on their right hand or forehead in order to engage in
any commercial transactions. Those who refuse the mark are sum-
marily beheaded.

Sounds pretty incredible, doesn't it? But is it biblical…or just
exciting fiction?

Let's look carefully together at what the text of Scripture *does*
and *does not* say about the mark of the beast.

TRIBULATION TRADEMARK?

The core issue of the coming tribulation period will be, "Who has
the right to rule—God or Satan?" God will demonstrate unmistak-
ably to all creation that He alone has that right.

But for the first and only time in history, people will have a deadline for declaring their allegiance to Christ and the gospel. Throughout the past two thousand years, people have been at different stages in deciding for or against acceptance of the Good News. People accept or reject this message at various points of their lives: some in childhood, some as young adults, some at middle age, some as seniors. During the Tribulation period, the process will be accelerated or forced.

Because of the mark of the beast.

As a result, all humanity will be consciously, visibly divided into two segments. And the polarizing issue will be that mandatory mark.

The Bible teaches that the false prophet, who is the head of Antichrist's religious propaganda machine, will take the lead in the mark of the beast campaign (Revelation 13:11–18). Revelation 13:15 makes it clear that the key issue underlying this whole hand-or-forehead-mark business is "worship [of] the image of the beast." In other words, the infamous mark is simply a vehicle to force people to declare their allegiance—to the Antichrist or to Jesus Christ. All the peoples of earth will be separated into two camps. It will be impossible to take a position of neutrality or indecision. Scripture declares that those who do not receive the mark will be killed (20:4).

All classes of humanity will be forced to take sides: "the small and the great, and the rich and the poor, and the free men and the slaves" (13:16). Robert Thomas, a noted New Testament scholar, notes that this language "extends to all people of every civic rank,…all classes ranked according to wealth,…covers every cultural category,… The three expressions are a formula for universality."[1] The Bible is very specific: The false prophet will require a "mark" of loyalty and devotion to the beast, and it will be "on their right hand," not the left, "or on their forehead" (v. 16).

144 THE TRUTH BEHIND LEFT BEHIND

But what is this "mark"? What will it be like? Is it just symbolic? Will it be visible?

THE MEANING OF THE MARK

We find the word *mark* sprinkled throughout the Bible. In Leviticus, for example, it refers numerous times to a mark that renders the subject ceremonially unclean, usually related to leprosy. Clearly in these cases the mark is external and visible.

Interestingly, Ezekiel 9:4 uses *mark* similarly to the way it is used in Revelation: "And the LORD said to him, 'Go through the midst of the city, even through the midst of Jerusalem, and put *a mark on the foreheads* of the men who sigh and groan over all the abominations which are being committed in its midst.'" Here the mark was one of preservation, similar to the way the blood on the doorposts spared those in the Exodus from the death angel. In Ezekiel, the mark is placed visibly on the forehead, anticipating Revelation's use of the term.

Seven out of the eight instances of the word for *mark* or *sign*—*charagma* in the Greek New Testament—appear in Revelation and refer to "the mark of the beast" (13:16–17; 14:9, 11; 16:2; 19:20; 20:4). Robert Thomas explains how the word was used in ancient times.

> The mark must be some sort of branding similar to that given soldiers, slaves, and temple devotees in John's day. In Asia Minor, devotees of pagan religions delighted in the display of such a tattoo as an emblem of ownership by a certain god. In Egypt, Ptolemy Philopator I branded Jews, who submitted to registration, with an ivy leaf in recognition of their Dionysian worship (cf. 3 *Macc.*

2:29). This meaning resembles the long-time practice of carrying signs to advertise religious loyalties (cf. Isa. 44:5) and follows the habit of branding slaves with the name or special mark of their owners (cf. Gal. 6:17). *Charagma* ("Mark") was a term for the images or names of emperors on Roman coins, so it fittingly could apply to the beast's emblem put on people.[2]

But why would this future world ruler use such a designation at all? What's the point? Antichrist's use of the mark appears to be a parody of the plan of God, especially God's "sealing" of the 144,000 witnesses of Revelation 7. God's seal of His witnesses is most likely invisible and is for the purpose of protection from the Antichrist. On the other hand, Antichrist offers protection from the wrath of God—a promise he cannot deliver—and his mark is visible and external.[3] Since those receiving the mark of the beast take it willingly, it must be a point of pride to have, in essence, Satan as one's owner. Robert Thomas says that, "It will be visible and the point of recognition for all in subjection to the beast."[4]

Revelation 13:16 provides further support that the mark will be external and visible. The mark is placed "on" the right hand or forehead. The Greek preposition "on" (*epi*) in this verse means "upon" not "in." Whatever this mark is, it will be "upon" or "on" the outside of the right hand or forehead.

THE TREACHEROUS TICKET

In addition to serving as a visible indicator of devotion to Antichrist, the mark will be the required ticket for any commercial transaction during the last half of the Tribulation (Revelation 13:17). This has been the dream of every tyrant down through history—to so totally control his subjects that he alone decides who can buy and sell.

Renowned historian Sir William Ramsay notes that first century Roman Emperor "Domitian carried the theory of Imperial Divinity and the encouragement of 'delation' to the most extravagant point;...that in one way or another every Asian must stamp himself overtly and visibly as loyal, or be forthwith disqualified from participation in ordinary social life and trading."[5] A future Antichrist will perfect such a practice with the aid of modern technology.

Many through history have tried to mark particular groups of people for death. Yet there have always been ways for a certain number to escape. As technology becomes more advanced, however, the frightening potential will exist to close up virtually every means of escape. Just such a picture is supported by the Greek word *dunétai*—"should" or "might" (Revelation 13:17)—which is used to convey an idea of what can or cannot be done. The Antichrist will not allow anyone to buy or sell without the mark.

Control of the economy at the individual level through the mark fits hand in glove with the biblical picture of Antichrist's control of global commerce as outlined in Revelation 17 and 18. The mark is something visible that must be shown in order to carry out any business or commercial transaction. This is another evidence that the mark will be visible. If the merchants couldn't see it, how could it serve as a regulation on whom could buy and sell?

The second half of Revelation 13:17 describes the mark as "either the name of the beast or the number of his name." Specifically, this means that the "number of the beast's name is one and the same with the name.... The equivalence means that as a name, it is written in letters, but as a number, the name's equivalent is in numbers."[6]

The Antichrist's name will be expressed numerically as "666."

CALCULATING THE NUMBER

At this point in the prophecy (Revelation 13:18), the apostle John shifts from one who simply records what he sees to one who specifically advises his readers on how to interpret what has been reported.

A reading of Revelation demonstrates clearly that the wicked will not understand because of their rejection of Jesus Christ as Lord and Savior. By contrast, wisdom and understanding about the identity of Antichrist will be given to believers during the Tribulation so that they might steadfastly refuse this evil mark of ownership. The Bible doesn't mince words here; those who take the mark of the beast cannot be saved (Revelation 14:9–11; 16:2; 19:20; 20:4) and will spend eternity in the lake of fire. The fact that John provides insight and understanding to believers at this crucial point relating to a matter of eternal importance shows that God will provide the knowledge His people need to follow Him faithfully.

What does this wisdom and understanding allow the believer to do? The passage says he will be able to "calculate" (13:18). Calculate what?

He will be able to calculate the number of the beast.

The primary purpose for warning believers about the mark is to let them know that when in the form of numbers, the "name" of the beast will be 666. Because of this warning, and because of the insight God will give His people in these days of suffering and fear, believers will understand the urgency of rejecting any such mark on their hand or forehead…even if it means death.

Because of the cataclysmic events of those latter days—the Rapture, the plagues, the earthquakes, the forming of a one world government—those who have become believers during this terrible period of tribulation will understand the implications of the mark. Believers today, however, before the time of the Rapture or the Tribulation, need not be superstitious about the number 666. If our address, phone number, or zip code includes this number, we do not need to be afraid that some satanic or mystical power will attach itself to us. While we recognize that many occultists and satanists are attracted to 666 because of its relation to future evil, the number itself does not contain mystical powers or influence. To believe that it does would mean that a believer has fallen prey to superstition.

JUMPING THE GUN

Many have tried to figure out the identity of the Antichrist through numerical calculations. Such approaches will always fail and should not be attempted. Phone books are full of names that might add up to 666 if converted to numerical values. The wisdom of "counting the name" is not to be applied in our day, for that would be jumping the gun. It is a specific warning for those who will come to Christ during the Great Tribulation.

In 2 Thessalonians 2:6, Paul teaches that during the current church age the Antichrist is being restrained. Antichrist will not be "revealed" until "his time." The Holy Spirit's selection of the word *revealed* indicates that the identity of the Antichrist will be concealed until the time of his revelation at some point after the Rapture. For this reason, it is not possible to discover his identity before "his time." Revelation plainly tells us that when the time comes, the identity of Antichrist will be all too obvious to believers. The implication will be unmistakable and universally understood by all the Christians in that dreadful hour: Accepting the mark of the beast will mean rejecting Jesus Christ. Forever.

No suggestions or speculation concerning the identity of the

Antichrist based on 666 have had—or will have—any merit until the Tribulation period arrives.

Revelation 13:17–18 makes it plain that the number 666 will be the mark proposed for the right hand or forehead. No one in history has even proposed such a number in anything like tribulation conditions, so past guesses as to his identity can be nullified on this basis. Robert Thomas provides wise guidance in this area.

> The better part of wisdom is to be content that the identification is not yet available, but will be when the future false Christ ascends to his throne. The person to whom 666 applies must have been future to John's time, because John clearly meant the number to be recognizable to someone. If it was not discernible to his generation and those immediately following him—and it was not—the generation to whom it will be discernible must have lain (and still lies) in the future. Past generations have provided many illustrations of this future personage, but all past candidates have proven inadequate as fulfillments.[7]

TECHNOLOGY AND THE MARK

Some have suggested that the mark of the beast will be the universal product code, a chip implanted under the skin, or an invisible mark requiring scanning technology to recognize it. Such applications do not align with what the Bible actually says. The mark of the beast—666—is not cashless technology or biometrics. The Bible speaks precisely about what the mark will be.

Here are fourteen fundamental facts about Antichrist's mark. It will be:

1. the Antichrist's own mark, identified with his person.
2. the actual number 666, not a representation.
3. a mark, like a tattoo.
4. visible to the naked eye.
5. on you, not in you.
6. recognized, not questioned.
7. voluntary, not involuntary—or given through deception.
8. used after the Rapture, not before.
9. used in the second half of the Tribulation.
10. needed to buy and sell.
11. universally received by non-Christians, but universally rejected by true believers.
12. shows worship and allegiance to the Antichrist.
13. promoted by the false prophet.
14. the destiny of all receiving the mark will be eternal punishment in the lake of fire.

All too often, sincere students of prophecy have tried to tie the number directly to contemporary technology and its potential in an effort to demonstrate the relevance of their interpretation. To do so, however, is to put the proverbial cart before the horse. Prophecy and the Bible do not gain authority or legitimacy because of culture or technology.

While it is easy to see how the coming cashless society could play into the hands of an autocrat attempting to gain control of the world economy, we do *not* believe that this economic ID system can be singled out as a forerunner to the mark of the beast. We can be certain, however, that whatever modern technology is available at the time of the Antichrist's ascent will be employed for his evil purposes. It will be used by the Antichrist, in conjunction with the mark, to control all buying and selling (as mentioned in Revelation

13:17), and it is likely that chip implants, scan technology, and biometrics will be used to implement the Antichrist's cashless society as a tool to regulate and enforce his restrictive global policies.

As with other developments in our day, we see many trends setting the stage that will facilitate the future career of the Antichrist.

Where is he now? Only God knows.

And He isn't telling.

CHAPTER TEN

WORLD NEWS AND LEFT BEHIND

As we stated at the beginning, our purpose in writing this book is to show that the Left Behind series presents a solid, reliable view of the end times—a view we believe squares with what the Bible says about the end of this age.

As we prepare to move into the more detailed discussion of part 2, we hope we've made our case. We hope you can clearly see the facts behind the fiction—The Truth Behind Left Behind. We hope you agree that the Left Behind view of the end times is backed up by strong, biblical evidence. Even if you don't agree with every detail of the end times scenario in Left Behind, you can see that it's based on well-grounded biblical interpretation and also strongly corroborated by the greatest witnesses of the early church.

But there's one final point concerning the Left Behind view of the end times that we think needs to be presented. And it has to do with what is often called the "signs of the times." We believe that many of the events in our world today validate the picture that Tim LaHaye and Jerry Jenkins so skillfully paint in their novels.

Of course, we should never adopt a view of end time prophecy based on current events. We should never look in the newspaper, see what's happening in our world, and then go to the Bible and try to find a Scripture we can make fit with what we see. On the other hand, after we have developed a view of the end times that is consistent with Scripture, we can and should look around our world and see if any events seem to point toward what the Bible predicts.

When we look at our world today, we believe that many events strikingly foreshadow the basic scenario presented in Left Behind. Many people are beginning to notice a remarkable correspondence between the general direction, trend, and flow of world events and what the Bible predicted centuries ago.

Let's briefly scan the horizon of our troubled world today and see if there are any events that could be setting the stage for the biblical events portrayed in Left Behind.

THE TIMES OF THE SIGNS

In the 1990 revision of his bestselling book *Oil, Armageddon and the Middle East Crisis,* John Walvoord wrote the following timely words—words that have an even stronger application today than when he penned them over ten years ago.

> The world is like a stage being set for a great drama. The major actors are already in the wings waiting for their moment in history.... The prophetic play is about to begin. The Middle East today occupies the attention of world leaders. The world has now recognized the political and economic power in the hands of those who control the tremendous oil reserves of the area. Old friendships and alliances will be subject to change as European nations seek new alliances and agreements to protect themselves in a changing world situation....
>
> All the necessary historical developments have already taken place. The trend toward world government, begun with the United Nations in 1946, is preparing the way for the government of the end time....
>
> Most important, Israel is back in the land, organized

as a political state, and eager for her role in the end-time events. Today Israel desperately needs the covenant of peace promised in prophecy. Largely because of the demands of the Palestinians, Israel will not be able to achieve a satisfactory settlement in direct negotiations.[1]

Walvoord notes:

Russia is poised to the north of the Holy Land for entry in the end-time conflict. Egypt and other African countries have not abandoned their desire to attack Israel from the south. Red China in the east is now a military power great enough to field an army as large as that described in the book of Revelation. Each nation is prepared to play out its role in the final hours of history...the beginning of the prophetic drama that will lead to Armageddon. Since the stage is being set for this dramatic climax of the age, it must mean that Christ's coming for His own is very near. If there ever was an hour when men should consider their personal relationship to Jesus Christ, it is today. God is saying to this generation: "Prepare for the coming of the Lord."[2]

We couldn't agree more. God's Word for this generation is *"Prepare for the coming of the Lord."* Never before in human history has there been such a convergence of trends and developments that lead into the very end times matrix predicted in Scripture. And never before have world events had such an immediate, instantaneous impact. Events that decades ago would have taken months or even years to bring about change now take minutes. This incredible acceleration of impact and effect creates a sense in all of us that we are moving toward a great crisis.

DARK SHADOWS

We have all been outside on many occasions and looked down to see our shadow on the pavement in front of us.

Of course we all know that our shadow is not us. It's not our substance. In some ways it resembles us, but in many others ways, not at all.

Yet it is a sign.

For instance, when you see Mark Hitchcock's shadow, you can count on the fact that Mark Hitchcock is near at hand. It's a sign that he is coming. (Not very quickly, perhaps—especially if he happens to be jogging—but with great certainty!)

In the same way, coming events often cast their shadows upon this world before they arrive, functioning as what we know as "signs of the times."

It is happening right now as you read these words. Future events are casting their shadows before them. We believe there are seven primary discernible shadows on the ground right at this very moment. Consider this astonishing convergence of world happenings and headlines—all predicted in Scripture thousands of years ago!

1. After nineteen hundred years of exile, Israel is being regathered to her ancient homeland, in the first stages of the fulfillment of Bible prophecy. And all eyes are riveted on this tiny nation. This regathering is nothing short of miraculous and is the key to all the other events of the end times. *It's a shadow of what is coming.*

2. According to Zechariah 12:1–3, Jerusalem is "ground zero" for the end times. And what do we see every day in the newspaper? Jerusalem is at the center of all the Middle East negotiations. Jerusalem is the city at the hub

of everything. She is a jagged, heavy burden to the world—an unsolvable problem for the world's diplomats. *It's a shadow of a gathering storm.*

3. The Roman Empire, sixteen hundred years after being broken apart, is being reunited before our eyes in the European Union. The EU currently has fifteen member nations. More nations are petitioning for entrance. The total is expected to be twenty-seven nations by 2007. The Euro is the new currency. The EU is developing a new constitution. The stage is set for one man to come on the scene to take over the EU and fulfill the Bible's prophecies of a final world ruler over the reunited Roman empire (Daniel 7:8, 24–26). *It's a shadow of what will be.*

4. Militant Islam is the most dangerous force in the world today. These radicals, joined by Russia, would love nothing more than to pour into Israel and plunder her, as the Bible predicts in Ezekiel 38–39. *It's a shadow of great events on the horizon.*

5. Globalism is the new world order. The world is shrinking right before our eyes. For the first time in human history since the Tower of Babel in Genesis 11, the whole world could literally be ruled economically and politically by one man, as depicted in Revelation 13:1–18. *It's a shadow that's growing larger every day.*

6. The world yearns for someone to bring peace to the Palestinian-Israeli problem. There is a collective, almost desperate cry for peace in our world. And peace in the Middle East is international priority number one. According to Daniel 9:27, Antichrist bursts on the world stage by forging a peace agreement with Israel (Revelation 6:1–2). *It's a shadow of vast changes already on their way.*

7. Events in Iraq make the rise of the New Babylon, predicted in Scripture, seem more likely every day. Iraq has only been a modern nation since 1932. Oil wasn't discovered there until 1927. Yet this nation is already front and center in the world. Current geo-political conditions, in conjunction with the rich oil reserves surrounding Babylon, make it a perfect setting for Antichrist's economic capital. *It's a shadow right in front of us—with the reality already bearing down.*

In light of all these signs, the truth is that none of us knows how much time we have *personally* or *prophetically*.

Personally, we don't know if we will live to see tomorrow. God gives us no guarantee of another breath. Prophetically, Jesus could come today and all who don't know Him will be left behind.

The signs of the end are all around us, and while many people are searching for answers, most people are ignoring God's warnings.

REMEMBER HARRY TRUMAN

On one of those all-too-rare clear days in Portland, Oregon, you can look off toward the northeastern horizon and view what's left of Mt. Saint Helens. Before May 18, 1980, it was a conical, picture-perfect 9,677 foot, snow-capped mountain.

But on 8:31 of that momentous day in May, the mountain exploded with the force of thirty thousand atomic bombs, sending super-sonic concussive waves that flattened everything within 150 square miles. On the heels of that wave, a fifty-foot wall of mud and ash screamed down the mountain and into the surrounding forest land, burying everything in its path and changing the landscape forever.

Old Harry Truman, caretaker of a recreation lodge on Spirit Lake at the foot of the mountain, perished in that eruption.

But it's not as though he hadn't been warned.

The curmudgeonly eighty-three-year-old widower knew very well what the geologists had been predicting. He knew that multiple seismographs and every scrap of scientific evidence pointed toward a massive, apocalyptic explosion.

But Harry refused to take any heed. In spite of the pleas of rangers, neighbors, and family, the old man laughed it off. "Nobody knows more about this mountain than Harry," he told a national television audience, "and it don't dare blow up on him…." Harry went about his business at the lodge…feeding his sixteen cats, mowing his lawn, and planting petunias.

Nothing would move him. Nothing would budge him. He ignored the fact of ten thousand earthquakes in a period of two months. He shrugged his shoulders at the hundreds of steam blast explosions, and an ominous eighty-meter bulge on the mountain's north flank. Harry laughed and Harry scoffed.

And then it was too late.

Thirteen hundred feet of the mountains summit blew into the skies of the Pacific Northwest…and Harry Truman was buried under six hundred feet of volcanic material. He had heard all the warnings, he had seen all the signs, he could feel the earth shake beneath his very feet—but he refused to believe.

This may describe you right now. You see the signs all around you, but you are just trying to ignore them. You are going on with your life. If so, then the most important thing for you to do is to hear God's Word and be saved from the wrath to come.

MAKE SURE YOU'RE READY

Are you ready to meet the Lord when He comes? You can be. The Lord's plan for saving man from His sins is so easy that the Bible says we must become like little children to enter God's kingdom.

Becoming a child of God involves three important steps:

STEP 1: ADMIT

You must realize that you need to be saved. You must admit your need. How many sins did it take for Adam and Eve to be excluded forever from the Garden of Eden? Just one. Likewise, it only takes one sin to keep us out of God's heaven. And if we are honest, we all know that we have committed many sins against the Lord. Romans 3:23 tells the truth about us: "For all have sinned and fall short of the glory of God."

STEP 2: ACKNOWLEDGE

You must recognize and acknowledge that you need a Savior. You cannot save yourself. No amount of good works, effort, church attendance, or ritual can take away your sin: "For by grace you have been saved through faith; and that not of yourselves, it is the gift of God; not as a result of works, so that no one may boast" (Ephesians 2:8–9).

STEP 3: ACCEPT

You must receive or accept Jesus Christ as your personal Savior from sin. It's not enough just to know that you are a sinner and that you need a Savior. You must acknowledge that Jesus is the

Savior you need, that He died on the cross to take away your sins, and that He rose again on the third day. And you must receive Him by faith. You must take the free gift of eternal life God offers. "But as many as received Him [Jesus], to them He gave the right to become children of God" (John 1:12).

NOW IS THE DAY OF SALVATION

Why not bow your head right now and call upon the Lord, accepting Christ as your personal Savior? Do it now. Don't put it off. It will be the greatest decision you will ever make. When you receive Christ, God promises to give you the precious gift of eternal life. "He who believes in the Son has eternal life" (John 3:36). Believe in the Lord Jesus Christ and you will be saved.

There are no magic words that bring salvation. God knows your heart. But a simple prayer like this can be used to express your desire to accept Jesus Christ as your Savior who paid the price for your sins.

> *Lord, I admit that I'm a sinner and that I need a Savior. I know that I cannot save myself. I believe that Jesus is the Savior who died on the cross for my sins and rose again from the dead. I accept Him now to be my Savior and Lord. Thank You for giving me the free gift of eternal life.*

Our prayer is that everyone who reads this book will be ready when Jesus comes to meet us in the air.

Remember, it could be today!

PART TWO

FOUNDATIONS

A NOTE BEFORE YOU BEGIN PART TWO

We've just taken a high-flying overview of end-time events and how they relate to the landmark, bestselling Left Behind series.

If you've ever watched old war movies, you know very well that after an air campaign, it's time to send in the infantry. The ground troops move in, taking enemy territory mile by mile. These next three chapters are for the infantry. They are for those of you who really want a better view of the landscape up close and are willing to lace up your boots and march through some challenging country. It won't all be easy going! There is some mountainous terrain that may test your resolve (remember Teddy Roosevelt and San Juan Hill!) and your desire to learn all you can about end-time matters.

Even so, we strongly recommend that you keep reading. The following information may very well put to rest any lingering doubts you may have about the biblical accuracy and strong foundation for the novels by Tim LaHaye and Jerry Jenkins.

Are you ready to march? Are you prepared to learn more than the average Joe or Jane about these terribly important issues? Then turn the page and *finish* a book that may be more timely than any of us have imagined.

CHAPTER ELEVEN

HOW SHOULD WE INTERPRET BIBLE PROPHECY?

The Golden Rule of Biblical Interpretation: When the plain sense of Scripture makes common sense, seek no other sense; therefore, take every word at its primary, ordinary, usual, literal meaning unless the facts of the immediate context, studied in the light of related passages and axiomatic and fundamental truths, indicate clearly otherwise.[1]

DR. DAVID L. COOPER

In his book *End Times Fiction*, Gary DeMar ridicules Tim LaHaye's claim that he interpreted the Bible literally in connection with the Left Behind series. "Having made the claim that his method is based on literalism, LaHaye spends considerable time redefining what he means by literalism," complains Gary DeMar. "He does this so he can account for the many symbols in Revelation and other parts of the Bible that he doesn't interpret in terms of his literalism definition."[2]

Carl Olson suggests that "One of the most attractive features of dispensationalism is that it is a method of interpreting Scripture that appears to be logical, tidy, and all-encompassing."[3] (We will discuss dispensationalism in depth in the next chapter. Simply put, the authors of Left Behind are dispensationalists, meaning they believe what the Bible literally teaches.)

It is certainly true that those of us who believe in the Left Behind view of the end times also advocate the use of literal interpretation, not just for Bible prophecy, but when studying any part of the entire Bible. In fact, LaHaye has long championed Dr. Cooper's golden rule of biblical interpretation. "If you follow this rule, it is relatively easy to understand Scripture; if you ignore it, you will always be in error," declares LaHaye. "That is particularly true of the prophetic sections of Scripture."[4]

However, critics of the Left Behind view of the end times have distorted what LaHaye means by literal interpretation of prophecy. This matter of literal interpretation is the most important issue in determining whether the theology of Left Behind is true. Therefore, we will attempt in this chapter to provide a careful statement and discussion of this most vital concern.

LITERAL INTERPRETATION DEFINED

The dictionary defines *literal* as "belonging to letters." It also says literal interpretation involves an approach "based on the actual words in their ordinary meaning...not going beyond the facts."[5] *The Oxford English Dictionary* says, "Pertaining to the 'letter' (of Scripture); the distinctive epithet of that sense or interpretation (of the text) which is obtained by taking its words in their natural or customary meaning and applying the ordinary rules of grammar; opposed to *mystical, allegorical,* etc."[6]

Literal interpretation of the Bible simply means to explain the original sense, or meaning, of the Bible according to the normal and customary usages of its language.[7] How is this done? It can be accomplished only through grammatical (according to the rules of grammar), historical (consistent with the historical setting of the passage), and contextual (in accord with its context) methods of interpretation.

Literalism looks to the text, the actual words and phrases of a passage. Allegorical or nonliteral interpretation imports an idea not found specifically in the text of a passage. Thus, the opposite of *literal* interpretation is *allegorical* interpretation. As Bernard Ramm, in his classic and authoritative book on biblical interpretation, said, "The 'literal' directly opposes the 'allegorical.'"[8]

LITERAL INTERPRETATION ILLUSTRATED

At this point in our discussion we are talking about an overall approach to Bible interpretation, often called hermeneutics. For example, Isaiah 2:1–5 is a passage that many have interpreted allegorically instead of literally. As you read the passage below, make a mental note of whom Isaiah is addressing. What does the text actually say?

> The word which Isaiah the son of Amoz saw concerning Judah and Jerusalem.
> Now it will come about that in the last days the mountain of the house of the LORD will be established as the chief of the mountains, and will be raised above the hills; and all the nations will stream to it. And many peoples will come and say, "Come, let us go up to the mountain of the Lord, to the house of the God of Jacob; that He may teach us concerning His ways and that we may walk in His paths." For the law will go forth from Zion and the word of the LORD from Jerusalem. And He will judge between the nations, and will render decisions for many peoples; and they will hammer their swords into plowshares and their spears into pruning hooks. Nation will not lift up sword against nation, and never

again will they learn war. Come, house of Jacob, and let
us walk in the light of the LORD.

The text of this passage addresses "Judah and Jerusalem" (v. 1),
"Zion" and "Jerusalem," (v. 3), and the "house of Jacob" (v. 5). Yet
many allegorical interpreters read this passage and simply substitute "the church" for the aforementioned synonyms for Israel.
Nowhere does the text say anything about the church. Those who
read this passage and note that it is referring to historical Judah and
Jerusalem are interpreting the passage literally—that is, according
to what the letter of the text actually says. Those who say that it
refers to the church, or something similar, are interpreting the passage allegorically—that is, importing an idea about the text where
there is no basis for such a thought in the actual letters of the text.

Allegorical interpreters take phrases like "the mountain of the
house of the LORD," "all the nations will stream to it," "many
peoples," and "the house of the God of Jacob" and say that this passage is teaching the conversion of the Gentiles to the Christian
faith and their ingathering into the Christian church.[9] Such an
understanding is not found at all in this passage. Such ideas have
to be imported from outside the text. When this is done, it results
in a nonliteral interpretation.

A literal interpretation of this passage is given in the *Tim
LaHaye Prophecy Study Bible* as follows:

> Isaiah envisions the Kingdom Age, when the nations of
> the world will come to the Holy City (Jerusalem) to
> learn the ways of God. Christ Himself is the Judge who
> will direct the affairs of nations, and peace shall prevail.
> Then the instruments of war and bloodshed will be
> refashioned into instruments of peace and prosperity.[10]

This interpretation is literal since it understands Jerusalem to refer to Jerusalem, and so on. This is what is meant by the system of literal interpretation, or hermeneutics.

GRAMMATICAL-HISTORICAL INTERPRETATION

Charles Ryrie, an advocate of literal interpretation, notes that literal interpretation is the same as the grammatical-historical method of interpretation:

> It is sometimes called the principle of *grammatical-historical* interpretation since the meaning of each word is determined by grammatical and historical considerations. The principle might also be called *normal* interpretation since the literal meaning of words is the normal approach to their understanding in all languages. It might also be designated *plain* interpretation so that no one receives the mistaken notion that the literal principle rules out figures of speech.[11]

A breakdown of categories to consider within the system of literal interpretation include grammatical, historical, contextual, and semantics. Let's examine each of these categories more closely.

GRAMMATICAL

The grammatical aspect of literal interpretation considers the impact that grammar plays on a passage. This means that a student of the text should correctly analyze the grammatical relationships of words, phrases, and sentences to one another. Literal interpreter Dr. Roy Zuck writes:

> When we speak of interpreting the Bible grammatically, we are referring to the process of seeking to determine its meaning by ascertaining four things: (a) the meaning of words (lexicology), (b) the form of words (morphology), (c) the function of words (parts of speech), and (d) the relationships of words (syntax).[12]

Dr. Zuck has been teaching biblical interpretation for many years at Dallas Theological Seminary, and we recommend his book *Basic Bible Interpretation* as a great place to start for anyone interested in learning how to interpret the Bible. Dr. Zuck provides further amplification of the four areas he noted above:

> In the meaning of words (lexicology), we are concerned with (a) etymology—how words are derived and developed, (b) usage—how words are used by the same and other authors, (c) synonyms and antonyms—how similar and opposite words are used, and (d) context—how words are used in various contexts.
>
> In discussing the form of words (morphology) we are looking at how words are structured and how that affects their meaning. For example the word *eat* means something different from *ate,* though the same letters are used…. The function of words (parts of speech) considers what the various forms do. These include attention to subjects, verbs, objects, nouns,

and others.... The relationships of words (syntax) are the way words are related or put together to form phrases, clauses, and sentences.[13]

Even though the grammatical aspect of literal interpretation is just one of a number of areas, it lets us know that any interpretation conflicting with grammar is invalid. Grammar is an important and foundational aspect of literal interpretation.

Historical

Proper interpretation of the Bible means that the historical context must be taken into account. This aspect means that one must consider the historical setting and circumstances in which the books of the Bible were written. Dr. Tan explains:

> The proper concept of the historical in Bible interpretation is to view the Scriptures as written during given ages and cultures. Applications may then be drawn which are relevant to our times. For instance, the subject of meat offered to idols can only be interpreted from the historical and cultural setting of New Testament times. Principles to be drawn are relevant to us today.[14]

Contextual

"A passage taken out of context is a pretext." This slogan is certainly true! Yet one of the most common mistakes made by those who are found to have misinterpreted a passage in the Bible is that of taking a verse out of its divinely ordered context. Even though a sentence may be taken from the Bible, it is not the Word of God if it is placed into a context that changes the meaning from that which God intended in its original context.

Dr. Roy Zuck says, "The context in which a given Scripture passage is written influences how that passage is to be understood. Context includes several things:

- the verse(s) immediately before and after a passage
- the paragraph and book in which the verses occur
- the dispensation in which it was written
- the message of the entire Bible
- the historical-cultural environment of that time when it was written."[15]

An example of a passage often taken out of context is Proverbs 11:30, which says, "The fruit of the righteous is a tree of life, and he who is wise wins souls." This is sometimes used as a verse to advocate evangelism. We are all for anyone who preaches the gospel to the lost. But when studied in context, the wise one who wins souls is someone who is able to draw others to himself and teach them wisdom. Wisdom, as used in Proverbs, refers to skill in everyday living. New Testament Christian evangelism is nowhere to be found in the context. If this passage is taken out of its context in Proverbs and the phrase "he who is wise wins souls" is placed by itself in a contemporary context, then it would be understandable that it could be thought to be advocating evangelism. However, such a meaning is impossible in its original context.

SEMANTICS

The principles of literal interpretation recognize that a biblical word or phrase may be used either plainly (denotative) or figuratively (connotative), just as in our own conversations today. For example, we might use plain speech to say, "He died yesterday" (denotative use of language). Or the same thing may be said in a more colorful way— "He kicked the bucket yesterday" (connotative use of language). Every word or phrase in every language is used in at least one of these two ways.

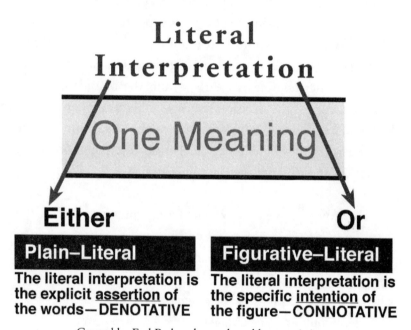

Created by Earl Radmacher and used by permission.

It is important to realize that even though we may use a figure of speech to refer to someone's death, we are using that word or phrase to refer to an event that literally occurred. Some interpreters are mistaken to think that just because a figure of speech may be used to describe an event (e.g., Jonah's description of his experience in the belly of the great fish in Jonah 2) that the event was not literal. Such is not the case.

Literal interpreters, for instance, understand that Isaiah is using a figure of speech in Isaiah 55:12. He is teaching that the Adamic curse upon nature will be reversed in the Millennium: "And all the trees of the field will clap their hands." This figure is discerned by specific factors in the context in which it was written. Trees don't have hands and thus do not clap. This figure of speech relates to the removal of the curse upon nature at a future time. Such an interpretation is supported by the preceding and subsequent contexts surrounding verse 12. That this is a figure of speech is decided by factors within the text itself. Such an understanding is clearly within the bounds of literal interpretation. If the decision about whether a tree can clap its hands was made on the basis of an idea imported from outside the text, then it would be an allegorical interpretation. Even though figurative language is employed, it will literally happen in history.

Therefore, we see that within the interpretative process the word *literal* is used in a second way, different from the first way in which we used it when referring to the system of *literal interpretation*. The second use of literal relates to the area of *semantics* and whether a word or phrase is used literally or figuratively. This is an important point to note because later we will demonstrate that this relates to how opponents of the Left Behind theology distort and misrepresent the literal interpretation of prophecy.

Dr. Ryrie drives this point home:

Symbols, figures of speech and types are all interpreted plainly in this method and they are in no way contrary to literal interpretation. After all, the very existence of any meaning for a figure of speech depends on the reality of the literal meaning of the terms involved. Figures often make the meaning plainer, but it is the literal, normal, or plain meaning that they convey to the reader.[16]

Notice that figures of speech are not a synonym for allegorical interpretation. Therefore, the presence of a figure of speech in a passage does not justify allegorical interpretation. Remember, allegorical interpretation involves the importing of an idea not actually stated by the words of the sentence into a text. A figure of speech is simply a connotative expression made by the words or phrases within the text itself.

DEMAR'S SHELL GAME

Left Behind theology opponent Gary DeMar uses a shell game to misrepresent and distort the literal interpretation of Tim LaHaye and the Left Behind theology. He attempts to make his point by arguing that since literal interpreters take some words and phrases as figures of speech, they are not consistent with literal interpretation. In *End Times Fiction,* DeMar truly redefines LaHaye's understanding and use of literal interpretation:

Throughout LaHaye's books on prophecy, especially his commentary on Revelation, we continually read why one thing after another is not to be interpreted literally (e.g., Revelation 12:1–2; 14:4). For example, while LaHaye states that "the word 'beast' is used thirty-four times in Revelation and many other times in Scripture," the word "is symbolic of either a king or kingdom (see Daniel 7–8)."[17] So then, these are not real beasts (animals). Why can't they be real flesh-and-blood beasts? As LaHaye states, "Is anything too hard for God?"[18] He insists that

174 THE TRUTH BEHIND LEFT BEHIND

God will make a chain strong enough to hold Satan
(Revelation 20:1). If so many things in Revelation are
symbolic, isn't it possible that the key and chain used to
bind Satan are also symbolic? Are there physical keys to
the kingdom of heaven (Matthew 16:19)? What about
the "keys of death and of hades" (Revelation 1:18)?

In Revelation 19:15 a sharp sword comes out of Jesus'
mouth to "smite the nations." But according to John
Walvoord, whom LaHaye quotes approvingly, the sword is
not literal. Rather, it represents "a sharp instrument of war,
with which Jesus will smite the nations and establish His
absolute rule."[19] Jesus is said to return on "a white horse"
(Revelation 19:11). If the horse is literal, then it conflicts
with Acts 1:11, which states, "This Jesus, who has been
taken up from you into heaven, will come in just the same
way as you have watched Him go into heaven." Jesus was
not taken to heaven on a horse (see Mark 16:19).

I could go on with even more examples, but you get
the point. LaHaye would claim that even "though some
prophetic passages should be interpreted symbolically, it is
important to remember that symbols in the Bible depict
real people, things, and events."[20] Once again, I agree. It's
my guess, however, that most Christians don't really
understand what LaHaye and other prophecy writers who
insist on literalism actually mean by the term when they
see it redefined this way. A sword is "a sharp instrument of
war" in Revelation 19, but a chain is a literal chain in
Revelation 20. Why can't they both be symbols?[21]

The above quote is an example of the shell game that DeMar
plays with LaHaye as he moves back and forth between the two

meanings of *literal.* The problem is that throughout DeMar's above cited passage, he is not using literalism in the same way LaHaye or anyone holding to the system of literal interpretation defines it. Instead, DeMar speaks of literalism as if LaHaye held to an approach often called "wooden literalism." Bernard Ramm, in his widely acclaimed book on biblical interpretation, writes, "The program of literal interpretation of Scripture does not over-look the figures of speech, the symbols, the types, the allegories that as a matter of fact are to be found in Holy Scripture. It is not a blind letterism nor a wooden literalism as is so often the accusation."[22]

DeMar evaluates LaHaye as if he should not ever take a word or phrase in the text of Scripture as a figure of speech or a symbol since LaHaye holds to literal interpretation. DeMar wrongly represents LaHaye's literalism as wooden literalism, though it is hard to understand why when, early in *End Times Fiction,* DeMar quotes LaHaye's statement of the golden rule of interpretation:

> The best guide to Bible study is "The Golden Rule of Biblical Interpretation." To depart from this rule opens the student to all forms of confusion and sometimes even heresy. When the plain sense of Scripture makes common sense, seek no other sense, but take every word at its primary, literal meaning unless the facts of the immediate context clearly indicate otherwise.[23]

Anyone can readily see, by reading the statement for themselves, that LaHaye's definition is within the clear framework of the classical literal interpretative approach. LaHaye says that words should be taken literally *"unless* the facts of the immediate context clearly indicate otherwise." DeMar performs an allegorical interpretation of LaHaye's statement by imposing an idea of wooden literalism from outside of that text.

PROPHETIC FULFILLMENT

One way that the literal interpretation of prophecy is vindicated is in examining how past prophecies were fulfilled. Paul Tan says that at "the first coming of Christ, over three hundred prophecies were completely fulfilled." Tan concludes that "every prophecy that has been fulfilled has been fulfilled literally. On the basis of New Testament attestations and the record of history, the fulfillment of Bible prophecy has always been literal."[24]

Ryrie also argues that the literal fulfillment of past prophecy means that future prophecy should be interpreted literally. He says, "The prophecies in the Old Testament concerning the first coming of Christ—His birth, His rearing, His ministry, His death, His resurrection—were all fulfilled literally. That argues strongly for the literal method."[25]

As early as the book of Genesis, God demonstrates that prophecy is fulfilled literally even when figures of speech and symbols are employed. A number of dreams and visions are depicted throughout Genesis in which God shows the future to some of His people. A classic example is found in Joseph's dreams about his ascendancy over his family in Genesis 37:5–12. In both dreams God uses symbols to convey the future. In one dream sheaves of grain represent Joseph and his brothers, while in the other dream the sun represents Jacob, the moon stands for Rachel, and the stars are his brothers. These dreams were literally fulfilled in the life of Joseph and his family as he later ruled over them when he rose to second in command over Egypt.

In Revelation 12, some of the prophetic symbols used are the same as those that appear in Joseph's prophetic dreams. Thus, in Revelation 12 the sun refers to Jacob, the moon stands for Rachel, and the stars are the twelve tribes of Israel. Even though symbols are used in Revelation 12, biblical precedent dictates that its prophecy should be interpreted literally and will be fulfilled literally as well.

CONCLUSION

As we noted at the beginning of this chapter, the issue of one's stand on the literal interpretation of prophecy will determine whether one agrees with the Left Behind view of the end times. The late John Walvoord, president of Dallas Theological Seminary for many decades, put it this way:

> The question of whether to interpret Scripture literally as opposed to non-literally is...a major controversy in the study of eschatology. Any student of prophetic Scripture must decide early whether prophecy should normally be understood by its literal meaning or in another way.[26]

We believe the biblical text does indeed teach the Left Behind theology. We believe that literal interpretation is the only valid way to interpret not just the Bible but all literature, and if that is the case, then it follows that the *Left Behind* view of the end times is biblical after all.[27]

CHAPTER TWELVE

WHAT IS DISPENSATIONALISM?

When discussion of the Left Behind view of the end times takes place among its opponents, you can be sure that the term *dispensationalism* will be used. In fact, many opponents of the Left Behind theology believe that dispensationalism is either downright heresy, or close to it. For many, dispensationalism has become a Christian cuss word!

Left Behind theology antagonist Carl Olson says:

> While the belief in the Rapture is largely based on
> 1 Thessalonians 4, dispensationalists also appeal to other
> verses from Scripture, including sections from
> 1 Corinthians 15, Revelation 3, and Matthew 24. These
> various texts are placed into an elaborate chronology of
> "end time" events based in the broader context of "dis-
> pensations," or era of time, usually seven in number. This
> system of historical division is broadly known as *dispensa-
> tionalism*.[1]

While dispensationalism is a term that does apply to those of us who believe in the Left Behind view of the end times, opponents have invested a great deal of time filling that word with invective and negativity, much of which is a distortion of reality.

So what is dispensationalism?

A CLUSTER OF ITEMS

Dispensationalism is a cluster of ideas joined together to form a system of thought, just as terms like *Calvinism, Arminianism, Anglicanism, Catholicism,* or *Lutheranism* are historical labels that represent not a single idea, but a group of ideas joined together to form a multifaceted scheme.

Dispensationalists are those who believe the following things:

- The Bible is God's inspired, inerrant (i.e., without any errors) revelation to man. Scripture provides the framework through which to interpret history (past and future). God's written Word tells us of His plan for His creation, and this will surely come to pass.
- Since the Bible is God's literal Word of His plan for history, it should be interpreted literally and historically (past and future).
- Since the Bible reveals God's plan for history, then it follows that there is an ebb and flow to His plan. Therefore, God's plan includes different dispensations, ages, or epochs of history through which His creatures (men and angels) are tested. Therefore, God is instructing His creatures through the progress of history.
- Since all humanity fell into sin, each person must individually receive God's provision of salvation through the death of Christ by believing the gospel. Thus, Jesus Christ is the only way to a relationship with God.
- Because of mankind's fall into sin, Scripture teaches that all humanity is naturally rebellious to God and the things of God. This is why only genuine believers in Christ are open to the teachings of the Bible. Thus, salvation

through Christ is a prerequisite to properly understanding God's Word.

- God's plan for history includes a purpose for the descendants of Abraham, Isaac, and Jacob—that is, Israel. This plan for Israel includes promises that they will have the land of Israel, will have a seed, and will be a worldwide blessing to the nations. Many of the promises to national Israel are yet future; therefore, God is not finished with Israel.

- God's plan from all eternity also includes a purpose for the church; however, this is a temporary phase that will end with the Rapture. After the Rapture, God will complete His plan for Israel and the Gentiles.

- The main purpose in God's master plan for history is to glorify Himself through Jesus Christ. Therefore, Jesus Christ is the goal and hero of history.

Christians who believe in this way are known as dispensationalists. Tim LaHaye, Jerry Jenkins, and the authors of this book are dispensationalists. Millions of Christians throughout the world are also dispensationalists. We believe that this is the same as saying that we believe what the Bible literally teaches.

A DEFINITION OF DISPENSATIONALISM

The leading spokesman for dispensationalism may be retired Dallas Theological Seminary professor Charles Ryrie. Many know Ryrie through his books and articles and the popular *Ryrie Study Bible*. Ryrie's book *Dispensationalism* is a primary reference point for gaining an understanding of dispensationalism.

Ryrie notes that *The Oxford English Dictionary* defines a theological dispensation as "a stage in a progressive revelation, expressly adapted to the needs of a particular nation or period of time.... Also, the age or period during which a system has prevailed."[2]

The English word *dispensation* is translated from the Greek noun *oikonomía*, often rendered "administration" in modern translations. The word *oikonomía* is a compound of *oíkos*, meaning "house," and *nómos*, meaning "law." Taken together, "the central idea in the word *dispensation* is that of managing or administering the affairs of a household."[3]

> The various forms of the word *dispensation* appear in the New Testament twenty times. The verb *oikonoméô* is used once in Luke 16:2, where it is translated "to be a steward." The noun *oikonómos* appears ten times (Luke 12:42; 16:1, 3, 8; Romans 16:23; 1 Corinthians 4:1–2; Galatians 4:2; Titus 1:7; 1 Peter 4:10) and is usually translated "steward" or "manager" (but "treasurer" in Romans 16:23). The noun *oikonomía* is used nine times (Luke 16:2–4; 1 Corinthians 9:17; Ephesians 1:10; 3:2, 9; Colossians 1:25; 1 Timothy 1:4). In these instances it is translated variously ("stewardship," "dispensation," "administration," "job," "commission").[4]

Further examination of *oikonómos* as it is used in the Gospels finds Christ using the word in two parables in Luke 12 and 16. Ryrie notes that in Luke 16 we find some important characteristics of a stewardship, or dispensational, arrangement:

1. Basically there are two parties: the one whose authority it is to delegate duties, and the one whose responsibility it is to carry out these charges. The rich man (or manager) plays these roles in the parable of Luke 16 (v. 1).

2. These are specific responsibilities. In the parable, the steward failed in his known duties when he wasted the goods of his lord (v. 1).

3. Accountability, as well as responsibility, is part of the arrangement. A steward may be called to account for the discharge of his stewardship at any time, for it is the owner's or master's prerogative to expect faithful obedience to the duties entrusted to the steward (v. 2).

4. A change may be made at any time unfaithfulness is found in the existing administration ("can no longer be steward").[5]

Further defining features can be gleaned from other occurrences of the *dispensation* word group. All other uses, except 1 Peter 4:10, are found in the writings of Paul. Ryrie cites the following features:

1. God is the one to whom men are responsible in the discharge of their stewardship obligations. In three instances this relationship to God is mentioned by Paul (1 Corinthians 4:1–2; Titus 1:7).

2. Faithfulness is required of those to whom a dispensational responsibility is committed (1 Corinthians 4:2). This is illustrated by Erastus, who held the important position of treasurer (steward) of the city (Romans 16:23).

3. A stewardship may end at an appointed time (Galatians 4:2). In this reference the end of the stewardship came because of a different purpose being introduced. This reference also shows that a dispensation is connected with time.

4. Dispensations are connected with the mysteries of God, that is, with specific revelation from God (1 Corinthians 4:1; Ephesians 3:2; Colossians 1:25).

5. Dispensation and age are connected ideas, but the words are not exactly interchangeable. For instance, Paul declares that the revelation of the present dispensation was hidden "for ages," meaning simply a long period of time (Ephesians 3:9). The same thing is said in Colossians 1:26. However, since a dispensation operates within a time period, the concepts are related.

6. At least three dispensations (as commonly understood in dispensational teaching) are mentioned by Paul. In Ephesians 1:10 he writes of "an administration [dispensation, KJV] suitable to the fullness of the times," which is a future period. In Ephesians 3:2, he designates the "stewardship [dispensation, KJV] of God's grace," which was the emphasis of the content of his preaching at that time. In Colossians 1:25–26 it is implied that another dispensation preceded the present one, in which the mystery of Christ in the believer is revealed.[6]

It should be noted that dispensationalists have developed the theological term *dispensation* in a way similar to the biblical use of the term. Therefore, we believe that the system of theology we know today as dispensationalism is consistent with biblical teaching.

Building upon these biblical observations, we are now able to define dispensationalism. According to Ryrie, "A dispensation is a distinguishable economy in the outworking of God's purpose." Ryrie notes concerning a dispensation that "the distinguishing features are introduced by God; the similar features are retained by

God; and the overall combined purpose of the whole program is the glory of God.[7]

In his classic work *Dispensationalism,* Ryrie formulates a more extensive definition of dispensationalism:

> Dispensationalism views the world as a household run by God. In this household-world God is dispensing or administering its affairs according to His own will and in various stages of revelation in the process of time. These various stages mark off the distinguishably different economies in the outworking of His total purpose, and these different economies constitute the dispensations. The understanding of God's differing economies is essential to a proper interpretation of His revelation within those various economies.[8]

Another dispensational scholar, Paul Nevin, summarizes dispensationalism as

> God's distinctive method of governing mankind or a group of men during a period of human history, marked by a crucial event, test, failure, and judgment. From the divine standpoint, it is an economy, or administration. From the human standpoint, it is a stewardship, a rule of life, or a responsibility for managing God's affairs in His house. From the historical standpoint, it is a stage in the progress of revelation.[9]

Dispensationalist Renald Showers, emphasizing a dispensational view of history, gives the following definition:

Dispensational Theology can be defined very simply as a system of theology which attempts to develop the Bible's philosophy of history on the basis of the sovereign rule of God. It represents the whole of Scripture and history as being covered by several dispensations of God's rule.... The term *dispensation* as it relates to Dispensational Theology could be defined as *a particular way of God's administering His rule over the world as He progressively works out His purpose for world history.*[10]

THE ESSENTIALS OF DISPENSATIONALISM

Essentials are needed by which to gauge a theology, but what are the essentials that characterize a dispensationalist? Ryrie has stated what he calls the three essentials, or *sine qua non* (Latin, "that without which"), of dispensationalism. The three essentials are not a definition or description of dispensationalism; instead they are basic theological tests that can be applied to an individual to determine whether or not he or she is a dispensationalist.

FIRST ESSENTIAL: LITERAL INTERPRETATION

Ryrie's first essential of dispensationalism is not just literal interpretation, but more fully, a *consistent* literal hermeneutic. "The word *literal* is perhaps not so good as either the word *normal* or *plain*," explains Ryrie, "but in any case it is interpretation that does not spiritualize or allegorize as nondispensational interpretation does."[11]

Literal interpretation is foundational to the dispensational approach to Scripture. Earl Radmacher went so far as to say that literal interpretation "is the 'bottom-line' of dispensationalism."[12]

SECOND ESSENTIAL: DISTINCTION BETWEEN ISRAEL AND THE CHURCH

"A dispensationalist keeps Israel and the church distinct," declares Ryrie. He also notes that anyone "who fails to distinguish Israel and the church consistently will inevitably not hold to dispensational distinctions; and one who does, will."[13]

What does Ryrie mean by keeping Israel and the church distinct? Dispensationalists believe the Bible teaches that God's single program for history includes a distinct plan for Israel and a distinct plan for the church. Lewis Sperry Chafer, founder and first president of Dallas Theological Seminary, has described the distinction as follows:

> The dispensationalist believes that throughout the ages God is pursuing two distinct purposes: one related to the earth with earthly people and earthly objectives involved which is Judaism; while the other is related to heaven with heavenly people and heavenly objectives involved, which is Christianity.[14]

If the unfulfilled promises given to Israel in the Old Testament literally refer to the Jews, then it is clear that God's plan for the people of Israel, who are currently in dispersion (see Deuteronomy 4:27–28; 28:63–68; 30:2–4), is on hold until He completes His current purpose with the church—which is to take out from the Gentiles a people for His name (see Acts 15:14)—and raptures the bride of Christ to heaven. After the Rapture, God will then complete His unfinished business with Israel (see Acts 15:16–18) during the seven-year Tribulation period. Thus, if one does not distinguish between passages in which God speaks to Israel and those intended for the church, the results will be an improper merging of the two programs.

In the Old Testament, God made certain promises to Abraham when He pledged to make him the father of a special people. Dispensationalists understand these promises, and other unconditional covenant promises (e.g., treaty grants) made by God to Israel, as still intact for Israel even though the church currently shares in some of Israel's spiritual blessings (see Romans 15:27). Ultimately God will not only restore Israel to a place of blessing (see Romans 11) but will also literally fulfill the land and kingdom promises made to Israel in the Abrahamic covenant (Genesis 12:1–3), Land of Israel covenant (Deuteronomy 30:1–10), and Davidic covenant (2 Samuel 7:12–16).

In the present time, God has another plan for the church that is distinct from His plan for Israel (Ephesians 2–3). Dispensationalists do not believe that the church is the New Israel or has replaced Israel as the heir to the Old Testament promises. Some nonliteralist scholars say that the church has superseded Israel, but nowhere in the New Testament is the church called Israel.

Dispensationalist Arnold Fruchtenbaum says:

> The conclusion is that the church is never called a "spiritual Israel" or a "new Israel." The term Israel is either used of the nation or the people as a whole, or of the believing remnant within. It is never used of the church in general or of Gentile believers in particular. In fact, even after the Cross there remains a threefold distinction. First, there is a distinction between Israel and the Gentiles as in 1 Corinthians 10:32 and Ephesians 2:11–12. Second, there is a distinction between Israel and the church in 1 Corinthians 10:32. Third, there is a distinction between Jewish believers (the Israel of God) and Gentile believers in Romans 9:6 and Galatians 6:16.[15]

THIRD ESSENTIAL: GLORY OF GOD IS THE PURPOSE OF HISTORY

The third essential of dispensationalism also revolves around another important distinction. Showers says this "indispensable factor is the recognition that the ultimate purpose of history is the glory of God through the demonstration that He alone is the sovereign God."[16]

Ryrie explains:

> We avow that the unifying principle of the Bible is the glory of God and that this is worked out in several ways—the program of redemption, the program for Israel, the punishment of the wicked, the plan for the angels, and the glory of God revealed through nature. We see all these programs as means of glorifying God, and we reject the charge that by distinguishing them (particularly God's program for Israel from His purpose for the church) we have bifurcated God's purpose.[17]

This essential is the most misunderstood and often thought to be the least essential. When properly understood, we believe that it is a valid essential. Dispensationalists are not saying that nondispensationalists do not believe in God's glory. We are making the point that the dispensationalist understanding of the plan of God is that He is glorified in history by more than just mankind's salvation (although this is probably the most important aspect of God's plan).

A BIBLICAL PHILOSOPHY OF HISTORY

Showers notes that a dispensational view of the Bible provides a believer with a biblical philosophy of history.[18] This is important for a Christian because when we understand God's purpose for each era of history, we are able to develop a worldview for living in accordance with God's will for each dispensation. A believer who has a divine perspective on the past, present, and future is better able to know what God expects of him in every area of life in our present day.

In the current church age, the New Testament instructs us in both private and public spheres of life. The dispensationalist, for example, does not live in this age of grace as if he were still under the rule of the Mosaic Law. Instead, we understand that we are now under the hundreds of commands that the New Testament calls the Law of Christ (1 Corinthians 9:21; Galatians 6:2). Current dispensational obligations are combined with responsibilities from previous ages, which continue in our own day, to provide a New Testament believer with a complete biblical framework for understanding how to please God in every area of our lives.

CONCLUSION

We believe that dispensationalism is a system of theology that has been properly developed from the Bible itself. Dispensationalism is essential to correctly understanding the Bible, especially biblical prophecy. No one will be able to rightly divide God's Word without understanding these great truths.

Ryrie concludes:

> If one does interpret the Bible this way, will it mean that he cuts out some of its parts? Not at all. Actually, the Bible comes alive as never before. There is no need to dodge the plain meaning of a passage or to reinterpret or spiritualize it in order to resolve conflicts with other passages. God's commands and standards for me today

become even more distinct, and His program with its unfolding splendor falls into a harmonious pattern. The history of dispensationalism is replete with men and women who love the Word of God and promote its study, and who have a burden for spreading the gospel to all the world.[19]

CHAPTER THIRTEEN

THE HISTORY OF THE RAPTURE

For several years opponents of the pre-Trib position have argued that it was invented by John Darby in the mid-1800s and was never mentioned before that. Quite simply, this argument is false—a fact that cost one post-Trib writer a bundle of cash. This author offered five hundred dollars to anyone who could prove that the pre-Trib Rapture theory was known before John Darby began to popularize it in the 1840s. When it was discovered that the Reverend Morgan Edwards saw it back in 1742, the writer had to pay off his costly challenge. He has since had to admit his error and withdraw his offer.[1]

TIM LAHAYE

Many of those who criticize the Left Behind theology always seem to raise some question about the history of the teaching of a pre-Tribulation Rapture. The argument is generally that since this teaching is less than two hundred years old, it cannot be biblical or Christians would have seen it many centuries earlier in church history. Gary DeMar declares, "All attempts to find a pre-Tribulation Rapture any earlier than around 1830 do not stand up to historical scrutiny."[2]

Is this claim true? If it were true, would that mean that the Left Behind theology is untrue? We will now take a quick journey through church history as we examine the history of the Rapture.

We need to deal with the history of the Rapture not because it is the basis for determining truth—that can be found only in Scripture—but because these issues are raised by critics of the Left Behind theology. Charles Ryrie has rightly said, "The fact that the church taught something in the first century does not make it true, and likewise if the church did not teach something until the twentieth century, it is not necessarily false."[3]

THE POST-APOSTOLIC CHURCH

That the earliest documents of the ancient church (in addition to the New Testament canon) reflect a clear premillennialism is generally conceded, but great controversy surrounds their understanding of the Rapture in relation to the Tribulation. Pretribulationists point to the early church's clear belief in imminency and a few passages from a couple of documents as evidence that pretribulationism was held by at least a few from the earliest times.

As was typical of every area of the early church's theology, their views of prophecy were undeveloped and sometimes contradictory, containing a seedbed out of which could develop various and diverse theological viewpoints. While it is hard to find clear pretribulationism spelled out among the fathers, there are clear pre-Trib elements, which if systematized with their other prophetic views contradict posttribulationism but support pretribulationism.

Since imminency is considered to be a crucial feature of pretribulationism by scholars such as John Walvoord,[4] it is significant that the apostolic fathers, though posttribulational, at the same time just as clearly taught the pretribulational feature of imminence.[5] Since it was common in the early church to hold contradictory positions without even an awareness of inconsistency, it would not be surprising to learn that their era supports both views. Larry Crutchfield notes, "This belief in the imminent return of Christ within the context of ongoing persecution has prompted us to broadly label the views of the earliest fathers 'imminent intra-Tribulationism.'"[6]

Expressions of imminency abound among the apostolic fathers. Clement of Rome, Ignatius of Antioch, *The Didache, The Epistle of Barnabas,* and *The Shepherd of Hermas* all speak of imminency.[7] Furthermore, *The Shepherd of Hermas* speaks of the pretribulational concept of escaping the Tribulation:

> You have escaped from great tribulation on account of your faith, and because you did not doubt in the presence of such a beast. Go, therefore, and tell the elect of the Lord His mighty deeds, and say to them that this beast is a type of the great tribulation that is coming. If then ye prepare yourselves, and repent with all your heart, and turn to the Lord, it will be possible for you to escape it, if your heart be pure and spotless, and ye spend the rest of the days of your life in serving the Lord blamelessly.[8]

Evidence of pre-Tribulationism surfaces during the early medieval period in a sermon some attribute to Ephraem the Syrian, but is more likely the product of one that scholars call Pseudo-Ephraem. The sermon, entitled *Sermon on the Last Times, the Antichrist, and the End of the World,* was written sometime between the fourth and sixth centuries.[9] The author's Rapture statement reads as follows:

> Why therefore do we not reject every care of earthly actions and prepare ourselves for the meeting of the Lord

Christ, so that he may draw us from the confusion,
which overwhelms all the world?... For all the saints and
elect of God are gathered, prior to the tribulation that is
to come, and are taken to the Lord lest they see the confusion that is to overwhelm the world because of our
sins.

This statement evidences a clear belief that all Christians will
escape the Tribulation through a gathering to the Lord and is stated
early in the sermon. How else can this be understood other than as
pretribulational? The later second coming of Christ to the earth
with the saints is mentioned at the end of the sermon. Gary
DeMar simply dismisses out of hand the Pseudo-Ephraem statement as a possible pre-Trib Rapture statement without giving any
reason.[10]

THE MEDIEVAL CHURCH

By the fifth century, the amillennialism of Origen and Augustine
had won the day in the established church, East and West. It is
probable that some form of premillennialism existed throughout
the Middle Ages, although primarily underground.

Dorothy deF. Abrahamse notes:

By medieval times the belief in an imminent apocalypse
had officially been relegated to the role of symbolic
theory by the Church; as early as the fourth century,
Augustine had declared that the Revelation of John was
to be interpreted symbolically rather than literally, and
for most of the Middle Ages Church councils and theologians considered only abstract eschatology to be

acceptable speculation. Since the nineteenth century, however, historians have recognized that *literal apocalypses did continue to circulate in the medieval world* and that they played a fundamental role in the creation of important strains of thought and legend.[11] (Italics added.)

It is believed that sects like the Albigenses, Lombards, and Waldenses were attracted to premillennialism, but little is known of the details of their beliefs since the Catholics destroyed their works when they were found. But there was at least one who held to some form of pretribulationism, namely one Brother Dolcino in 1304.

Francis Gumerlock is one individual who advocates the Brother Dolcino find, which is interesting because he first announced this in a book published by critic Gary DeMar's organization American Vision.[12] In fact, DeMar wrote a glowing foreword to Gumerlock's book. In his book *The Day and the Hour,* Gumerlock said the following: "The Dolicinites held to a pre-Tribulation rapture theory similar to that in modern dispensationalism."[13]

Gumerlock hits the nail on the head when he says of Brother Dolcino's Rapture teaching, "It challenges evangelicals to reevaluate their thinking about the history of the pre-Tribulational Rapture, especially those views which place the origin of the teaching, or its initial recovery, within the last two hundred years."[14]

The reason Gumerlock believes that Brother Dolcino taught pretribulationism is found in the following statement:

[Dolcino believed and preached and taught] that within those three years Dolcino himself and his followers will preach the coming of the Antichrist. And that the

Antichrist was coming into this world within the bounds of the said three and a half years; and after he had come, then *he [Dolcino] and his followers would be transferred into Paradise,* in which are Enoch and Elijah. And in this way they will be *preserved unharmed from the persecution of Antichrist.* And that then Enoch and Elijah themselves would descend on the earth for the purpose of preaching [against] Antichrist. Then they would be killed by him or by his servants, and thus *Antichrist would reign for a long time.* But when the Antichrist is dead, Dolcino himself, who then would be the holy pope, and his preserved followers, will descend on the earth, and will preach the right faith of Christ to all, and will convert those who will be living then to the true faith of Jesus Christ.[15]

Gumerlock clearly believes that this is a pre-Trib Rapture statement. He concludes:

This paragraph from *The History of Brother Dolcino* indicates that in northern Italy in the early fourteenth century a teaching very similar to modern pre-Tribulationalism was being preached. Responding to distressing political and ecclesiastical conditions, Dolcino engaged in detailed speculations about eschatology and believed that the coming of the Antichrist was imminent. He also believed that the means by which God would protect His people from the persecution of the Antichrist would be through a translation of the saints to paradise.[16]

THE REFORMATION CHURCH

After over a thousand years of suppression by the Catholic church, the concept of premillennialism began to be revived as a result of at least four factors. First, the Reformers went back to the sources, which for them were the Bible and apostolic fathers. This exposed them to an orthodox premillennialism. Specifically significant was the reappearance of the full text of Irenaeus's *Against Heresies*, which included the last five chapters that espouse a consistent futurism and cast the seventieth week of Daniel into the future.

Second, the Reformers repudiated much of the allegorization that dominated medieval hermeneutics by adopting a more literal approach, especially in the area of the historical exegesis.

Third, many of the Protestants came into contact with Jews and learned Hebrew. This raised concerns over whether passages that speak of national Israel were to be taken historically or continued to be allegorized within the tradition of the Middle Ages. The more the Reformers took them as historical, the more they were awakened to premillennial interpretations, in spite of the fact that they were often labeled "Judaizers."

Fourth, beginning in the late fifteenth century, the translation of the Bible into the native tongues of the people (for the first time since the days of the early church) produced an explosion of Bible reading. This resulted in a general knowledge of the Bible, especially the Old Testament, for the first time in church history. Since the Old Testament speaks primarily of Israel, it took just a few decades for people to start thinking about Israel and her future. This also contributed to a revival of premillennialism.

By the late 1500s and the early 1600s, premillennialism began to return as a factor within the mainstream church after more than a thousand years of amillennialism. With the flowering of biblical interpretation during the late Reformation period, premillennial interpreters began to abound throughout Protestantism, and so did the developing interest in the Rapture.

It has been claimed that some separated the Rapture from the Second Coming as early as Joseph Mede, who with his seminal work *Clavis Apocalyptica* in 1627, is considered the father of English premillennialism.

Paul Boyer says that Increase Mather proved "that the saints would 'be *caught up into the Air*' beforehand, thereby escaping the final conflagration—an early formulation of the Rapture doctrine more fully elaborated in the nineteenth century."[17]

Whatever these men were saying, it is clear that the application of a more literal hermeneutic was leading to a distinction between the Rapture and the Second Coming as separate events.

Others began to speak of the Rapture. Paul Benware notes:

Peter Jurieu in his book *Approaching Deliverance of the Church* (1687) taught that Christ would come in the air to rapture the saints and return to heaven before the battle of Armageddon. He spoke of a secret Rapture prior to His coming in glory and judgment at Armageddon. Philip Doddridge's commentary on the New Testament (1738) and John Gill's commentary on the New Testament (1748) both use the term *rapture* and speak of it as imminent. It is clear that these men believed that this coming will precede Christ's descent to the earth and the time of judgment. The purpose was to preserve believers from the time of judgment. James Macknight (1763) and Thomas Scott (1792) taught that the righteous will be carried to heaven, where they will be secure until the time of judgment is over.[18]

Researcher Frank Marotta believes that Thomas Collier in 1674 made reference to a pretribulational rapture, but rejected the view,[19] thus showing his awareness that such a view was being taught in the late seventeenth century. There is the interesting case of John Asgill, who wrote a book in 1700 about the possibility of translation (i.e., Rapture) without seeing death.[20] As a result of writing this book, Asgill was removed from the Irish parliament in 1703 and then from the English parliament in 1707. "His book had been examined and pronounced blasphemous, and had been burnt by order of the House without his having been heard in its defense."[21] Asgill spent the last thirty years of his life in prison because of his book, which would tend to throw cold water on anyone desiring to make known their thoughts on the Rapture.

Perhaps the clearest reference to a pre-Trib Rapture before Darby comes from Baptist Morgan Edwards, founder of Brown University, who saw a distinct Rapture three and a half years before the start of the Millennium.[22] The discovery of Edwards, who wrote about his pre-Trib beliefs in 1744 and later published them in 1788, is hard to dismiss:

> *The distance between the first and second resurrection will be somewhat more than a thousand years.* I say, *somewhat more—*, because the dead saints will be raised, and the living changed at Christ's "appearing in the air" (1 Thessalonians 4:17); and *this will be about three years and a half before the millennium,* as we shall see hereafter: but will he and they abide in the air all that time? No: they will ascend to paradise, or to some one of those many "mansions in the father's house" (John 14:2), and *disappear during the foresaid period of time.* The design of this retreat and disappearing will be to judge the risen and

changed saints; for "now the time is come that judgment must begin," and that will be "at the house of God" (1 Peter 4:17).[23]

Edwards clearly separates the Rapture from the Second Coming by three and a half years. He uses pre-Trib verses like 1 Thessalonians 4:17 and John 14:2 to describe the Rapture. He, like modern pretribulationists, links the time in heaven during the Tribulation with the "bema" judgment of believers.

The only difference, at least as far as the above statements go, between current pretribulationism and Edwards is the time interval of three and a half years instead of seven. This does not mean, however, that Edwards is a midtribulationist, since it appears that he thought the totality of the Tribulation was three and a half, not seven, years.

THE MODERN CHURCH

As futurism began to replace historicism within premillennial circles in the 1820s, the modern proponent of dispensational pretribulationism arrived on the scene. J. N. Darby claimed to have first understood his view of the Rapture as the result of Bible study during a convalescence from December 1826 until January 1827.[24] His work is the fountainhead for the modern version of the doctrine.

The doctrine of the Rapture spread around the world through the Brethren movement with which Darby and other like-minded Christians were associated. It appears that either through their writings or personal visits to North America, this version of pretribulationism was spread throughout American evangelicalism. Two early proponents of the view include Presbyterian James H. Brookes and Baptist J. R. Graves.

The Rapture was further spread through annual Bible conferences such as the Niagara Bible Conference (1878–1909); turn of the century publications like *The Truth* and *Our Hope;* popular books like Brookes's *Maranatha*; William Blackstone's *Jesus Is Coming*; and *The Scofield Reference Bible* (1909). Many of the greatest Bible teachers of the first half of the twentieth century helped spread the doctrine—among them, Arno Gaebelein, C. I. Scofield, A. J. Gordon, James M. Gray, R. A. Torrey, Harry Ironside, and Lewis S. Chafer.

During this time in virtually every major metropolitan area in North America, a Bible institute, Bible college, or seminary was founded that expounded dispensational pretribulationism. Schools like Moody Bible Institute, the Philadelphia Bible College, Bible Institute of Los Angeles (BIOLA), and Dallas Theological Seminary taught and defended these views. These teachings were found primarily in independent churches, Bible churches, Baptist churches, and a significant number of Presbyterian churches. Around 1925, pretribulationism was adopted by many Pentecostal denominations, such as the Assemblies of God and the Foursquare Gospel denomination. Pretribulationism was dominate among charismatics in the 1960s and 1970s. Hal Lindsey's *The Late Great Planet Earth* (1970) furthered the spread of the pre-Trib Rapture as it exerted great influence throughout popular American culture and then around the world. Many radio and television programs also began teaching pretribulationism.

FALSE CLAIMS OF RAPTURE ORIGINS

Dave MacPherson has made a living during the last thirty-five years by espousing conspiracy theories about the origin of pretribulationism.[25] He is the source of the claim that pretribulationism was invented by a fifteen-year-old girl named Margaret Macdonald from Port Glasgow, Scotland. There are a number of reasons why this cannot be true.

First, it is doubtful that Margaret Macdonald's "prophecy" contains any elements related to the pre-Trib rapture.[26] Second, no one has ever demonstrated *from actual facts of history* that Darby was influenced by Macdonald's "prophecy," even if it had contained pre-Trib elements, which it did not.[27]

John Walvoord has said:

> The whole controversy as aroused by Dave MacPherson's claims has so little supporting evidence, despite his careful research, that one wonders how he can write his book with a straight face. Pre-Tribulationalists should be indebted to Dave MacPherson for exposing the facts, namely, that there is no proof that MacDonald [sic] or Irving originated the pre-Tribulation rapture teaching.[28]

In fact, J. N. Darby clearly held to an early form of the pre-Trib Rapture in January 1827—a full three years before MacPherson's claim of 1830.

Brethren writer Roy A. Huebner claims and *documents* his belief that Darby first began to believe in the pre-Trib Rapture and develop his dispensational thinking while convalescing from a riding accident in December 1826.[29] If this is true, then all the origin-of-the-Rapture conspiracy theories fall to the ground in a heap of speculative rubble. Huebner provides clarification and evidence that Darby was not influenced by a fifteen-year-old girl, Lacunza, Edward Irving, or the Irvingites—all of whom are said by detractors of the pre-Trib Rapture to be bridges that led to Darby's thought—but that Darby's understanding of the Rapture was the product of his personal interaction with the text of Scripture, as he contended.

Darby's pre-Trib and dispensational thoughts, says Huebner, were developed from the following factors:

1. He saw from Isaiah 32 that there was a different dispensation coming and that Israel and the church were distinct entities.[30]

2. During his convalescence, Darby learned that he ought daily to expect his Lord's return.[31]

3. He came to understand the fall, or "ruin," of the church.[32]

4. Darby was beginning to see a gap of time between the Rapture and the Second Coming by 1827.[33]

5. Darby himself said in 1857 that he first started understanding things relating to the pre-Trib Rapture "thirty years ago." With that fixed point of reference, we can see that Darby had already understood the truths upon which the pre-Tribulation Rapture hinges.[34]

When reading Darby's earliest published essay on biblical prophecy (1829), it is clear that while it still has elements of historicism, it also reflects the fact that, for Darby, the Rapture was to be the church's focus and hope.[35] Even in this earliest of essays, Darby expounds upon the Rapture as the church's hope.[36]

The various "Rapture origin" theories espoused by opponents of pretribulationism are not accepted as historically valid by scholars who have examined the evidence. Clearly, MacPherson has not proven his point.

Historian Timothy P. Weber's evaluation is as follows:

> The pretribulation rapture was a neat solution to a
> thorny problem and historians are still trying to deter-
> mine how or where Darby got it.... A newer though still
> not totally convincing view contends that the doctrine
> initially appeared in a prophetic vision of Margaret
> Macdonald.... Possibly, we may have to settle for Darby's
> own explanation.[37]

American historian Richard R. Reiter informs us that "[Robert] Cameron probably traced this important but apparently erroneous view back to S. P. Tregelles." Reiter noted that historian Ian S. Rennie regarded McPherson's case as "interesting but not conclusive."[38]

Posttribulationist William E. Bell asserts, "It seems only fair, however, in the absence of eyewitnesses to settle the argument conclusively, that the benefit of the doubt should be given to Darby, and that the charge made by Tregelles be regarded as a possibility but with insufficient support to merit its acceptance.... This conclusion is greatly strengthened by Darby's own claim to have arrived at the doctrine through his study of 2 Thessalonians 2:1–2."[39]

Huebner considers MacPherson's charges as "slander that J. N. Darby took the (truth of the) pre-Tribulation Rapture from those very opposing, demon-inspired utterances."[40] He goes on to conclude that MacPherson "did not profit by reading the utterances allegedly by Miss M. M. Instead of apprehending the plain import of her statements, as given by R. Norton, which has some affinity to the post-tribulation scheme and no real resemblance to the pre-Tribulation Rapture and dispensational truth, he has read into it what he appears so anxious to find."[41]

IRVINGITES AND THE RAPTURE

One of Dave McPherson's strangest claims is that Edward Irving and the Irvingites taught a pre-Tribulation Rapture. The Irvingites are said by McPherson to be the source from which Darby clandestinely stole the doctrine and then claimed it as his own discovery.[42]

But Columba G. Flegg notes:

> There were…very significant differences between the two eschatologies, and attempts to see any direct influence of one upon the other seem unlikely to succeed—they had a number of common *roots*, but are much more notable for their points of disagreement. Several writers have attempted to trace Darby's secret rapture theory to a prophetic statement associated with Irving, but their arguments do not stand up to serious criticism.[43]

Other scholars who have researched in depth Irvingite views of Bible prophecy agree with Flegg's conclusion that the Irvingites never held to pretribulationism. Grayson Carter declares, "Nor can Darby's concept of a *secret* 'rapture'…be found in the teachings of Irving or any member of the Catholic Apostolics."[44]

When reading the full message of Irvingite eschatology, it is clear that they were still very much locked into a "historicist" system, which views the entire church age as the Tribulation. After all, the major point in Irving's eschatology was that Babylon (false Christianity) was about to be destroyed and then the Second Coming would occur. He also taught that the Second Coming was synonymous with the Rapture.[45] Irving believed that raptured saints would stay in heaven until the earth was renovated by fire and then return to the earth. This is hardly pre-Trib doctrine since Irving believed that the Tribulation began at least fifteen hundred years earlier and that he did not teach a separate Rapture, followed by the Tribulation, culminating in the Second Coming.

CONCLUSION

So where did Darby come up with the pre-Tribulation Rapture? John Walvoord's assessment is likely close to the truth:

> Any careful student of Darby soon discovers that he did not get his eschatological views from men, but rather from his doctrine of the church as the body of Christ, a concept no one claims was revealed supernaturally to Irving or Macdonald. Darby's views undoubtedly were gradually formed, but they were theologically and biblically based rather than derived from Irving's pre-Pentecostal group.[46]

While it is true that modern pretribulationism sprang from Darby's teaching, it is far from the truth to say that the Rapture was not taught before the 1800s. Belief in the blessed hope of the Rapture has often flourished throughout the history of the church when the freedom to study and propagate the teachings of Scripture prevailed.

The publisher and author would love to hear your comments about this book. *Please contact us at:*
www.multnomah.net/truthbehindleftbehind

NOTES

INTRODUCTION

1. See the testimonies in Tim LaHaye and Jerry B. Jenkins, with Norman B. Rohrer, *These Will Not Be Left Behind: True Stories of Changed Lives* (Wheaton, IL: Tyndale House, 2003).
2. For a refutation of preterism, see Tim LaHaye and Thomas Ice, eds., *The End Time Controversy: The Second Coming Under Attack* (Eugene, OR: Harvest House, 2003).

CHAPTER ONE

1. Here are just a couple of examples: Samuele Bacchiocchi, "Left Behind: Fact or Fiction?" *Endtimes Issues* no. 62 (revised), March 28, 2001. http://www.biblicalperspectives.com/endtimeissues/eti_62.pdf (accessed November 11, 2003); Charles Henderson, "The Left Behind Series: Bad Fiction, Bad Faith," *About,* http://christianity.about.com/cs/adultchristianity/a/leftbehind.htm (accessed November 11, 2003).
2. At the 213th General Assembly of the Presbyterian Church (USA), Overture 01-25 passed. This Overture states that pastors in Presbyterian USA churches are to communicate to their congregations that the Left Behind series is not in accord with their interpretation of the Bible, especially the book of Revelation. "Rooted and Grounded in Love: 213th General Assembly," *Presbyterian Church USA,* http://www.pcusa.org/ga213/business/OVT0125.htm (accessed November 19, 2003).
3. David Cloud, a fundamental Baptist, takes serious issue with the Left Behind view of people being saved after the Rapture. "Left Behind: Tolerable Entertainment, Intolerable Theology," *Way of Life Literature* (2001) http://www.wayoflife.org/fbns/leftbehind.htm (accessed November 11, 2003).
4. Some of the harshest, most strident criticism of Left Behind has come from Roman Catholics. See Cathleen Falsani, "Bishops Warn Catholics About 'Left Behind' Books," *Chicago Sun-Times,* June 6, 2003.

CHAPTER TWO

1. Carl E. Olson, *Will Catholics Be "Left Behind"? A Catholic Critique of the Rapture and Today's Prophecy Preachers* (San Francisco: Ignatius Press, 2003), 290.
2. Gary DeMar, *End Times Fiction: A Biblical Consideration of the Left Behind Theology* (Nashville: Thomas Nelson, 2001), 17.
3. Paul Thigpen, *The Rapture Trap: A Catholic Response to "End Times" Fever* (West Chester, PA: Ascension Press, 2002), 30.
4. *The Compact Edition of the Oxford English Dictionary* (New York: Oxford Press, 1971), s.v., "Rapture."
5. Walter Bauer, William Arndt, and Wilbur Gingrich, *A Greek-English Lexicon of the New Testament and Other Early Christian Literature* (Chicago: University of Chicago Press, 1957), 108.
6. *Cassell's Latin Dictionary* (New York: MacMillan, 1968), 500–1.
7. John F. Walvoord, "Conclusion: Fifty Arguments for PreTribulationism," *Bibliotheca Sacra* 113 (July 1956): 193–9. Another important argument for the pre-Trib Rapture is the necessity of an interval between the Rapture and the Second Coming. An interval or gap of time

is needed between the Rapture and the Second Coming in order to facilitate many events predicted in the Bible in a timely manner. Numerous items in the New Testament can be harmonized by a pre-Trib time gap of at least seven years, while other views, especially post-Tribulationists, are forced to postulate scenarios that would not realistically allow for a normal passage of time. The following events are best harmonized with an interval of time as put forth by pretribulationism. Second Corinthians 5:10 teaches that all believers of this age must appear before the judgment seat of Christ in heaven. This event, often known as the "Bema Judgment" from the Greek word *bema,* is an event never mentioned in the detailed accounts connected with the second coming of Christ to the earth. Since such an evaluation would require some passage of time, the pre-Trib gap of seven years nicely accounts for such a requirement.

Since Revelation 19:7–10 pictures the church as a bride who has been made ready for marriage (illustrated as "fine linen," which represents "the righteous acts of the saints") to her groom (Christ), and since the bride has already been clothed in preparation for her return at the Second Coming accompanying Christ to the earth (Revelation 19:11–18), it follows that the church would already have to be complete and in heaven (because of the pre-Trib Rapture) in order to have been prepared in the way that Revelation 19 describes. This requires an interval of time which pretribulationism handles well.

Believers who come to faith in Christ during the Tribulation are not translated at Christ's second advent, but carry on ordinary occupations such as farming and building houses, and they will bear children (Isaiah 65:20–25). This would be impossible if all saints were translated at the Second Coming to the earth, as posttribulationists teach. Because pretribulationists have at least a seven-year interval between the removal of the church at the Rapture and the return of Christ to earth, this is not a problem—millions of people will be saved during the interval and thus will be available to populate the Millennium in their natural bodies in order to fulfill Scripture.

It would be impossible for the judgment of the Gentiles to take place after the Second Coming if the Rapture and Second Coming are not separated by a gap of time. How would both saved and unsaved, still in their natural bodies, be separated in judgment if all living believers are translated at the Second Coming? This would be impossible if the translation takes place at the Second Coming, but it is solved through a pretribulational gap.

Dr. John F. Walvoord points out that if "the translation took place in connection with the Second Coming to the earth, there would be no need of separating the sheep from the goats at a subsequent judgment, but the separation would have taken place in the very act of the translation of the believers before Christ actually sets up His throne on earth (Matthew 25:31)." John F. Walvoord, *The Rapture Question: Revised and Enlarged Edition* (Grand Rapids, MI: Zondervan, 1979), 274. Once again, such a "problem" is solved by taking a pre-Trib position with its gap of at least seven years.

A time interval is needed so that God's program for the church, a time when Jew and Gentile are united in one body (cf. Ephesians 2–3), will not become commingled in any way with His unfinished and future plan for Israel during the Tribulation. Dr. Renald Showers notes that "[A]ll other views of the Rapture have the church going through at least part of the 70th week, meaning that all other views mix God's 70-weeks program for Israel and Jerusalem together with His program for the church. A gap is needed in order for these two aspects of God's program to be harmonized in a non-conflicting manner." Renald Showers, *Maranatha Our Lord, Come! A Definitive Study of the Rapture of the Church* (Bellmawr, NJ: The Friends of Israel Gospel Ministry, 1995), 243.

The pretribulational Rapture of the church not only fulfills a biblical need to see a distinction between the translation of church age saints at the Rapture, before the Second

Coming, but it also handles without difficulty the necessity of a time gap that harmonizes a number of future biblical events. This requirement of a seven-year gap of time adds another plank to the likelihood that pretribulationism best reflects the biblical viewpoint.

8. Donald Grey Barnhouse, *Thessalonians: An Expositional Commentary* (Grand Rapids, MI: Zondervan, 1977), 99–100.

9. John F. Walvoord, *The Return of the Lord* (Grand Rapids, MI: Zondervan, 1955), 88. The quotation and the first six contrasts in the comparison above are taken from 87–8 of Walvoord's *The Return.*

10. Walvoord, *The Rapture Question,* 273.

CHAPTER THREE

1. Gary DeMar, *End Times Fiction: A Biblical Consideration of the Left Behind Theology* (Nashville: Thomas Nelson, 12–5.

2. Ibid., 13.

3. The Hebrew word *'acharith* (end, last, or latter) when used in reference to time means "latter part" or "close." The standard Hebrew lexicon says, "in the end of the days, a prophetic phrase denoting the final period of the history so far as the speaker's perspective reaches...it often equals the ideal or Messianic future." Francis Brown, *The New Brown—Driver—Briggs—Gesenius Hebrew and English Lexicon* (Peabody, MA: Hendrickson Publishers, 1979), 31. Horst Seebass says that the Hebrew term "last days" or "end of the days" (*'acharith hayyamim*) is a technical term in Daniel 2:28; 10:14; Hosea 3:5; and Ezekiel 38:16 not just for the future in general but for the end of time. He says it refers to "how history will culminate, thus its outcome." Horst Seabass, *Theological Dictionary of the Old Testament,* ed. G. Johannes Botterweck and Helmer Ringgren, trans. John T. Willis (Grand Rapids, MI: William B. Eerdmans Publishing Company, 1974), 211–2.

4. Concerning the possibility of a Russian/Islamic invasion of Israel in the end times, C. Marvin Pate and J. Daniel Hays say categorically, "The biblical term rosh has nothing to do with Russia" (69). And later they state dogmatically, "These positions are not biblical.... A world government is not coming to Babylon, and a Russian-led Muslim invasion of Israel is not about to take place." C. Marvin Pate and J. Daniel Hays, *Iraq—Babylon of the End Times?* (Grand Rapids, MI: Baker, 2003), 136.

5. The English translations that mistranslate *Rosh* as "chief" take their lead from the Latin Vulgate of Jerome. When Jerome made his translation, he had four Greek translations available, and three of them translated Rosh as a proper noun (Septuagint, Symmachus, and Theodotian). The translation of Aquila was the only one that translated it as an adjective. Jerome adopted this translation. However, in his Commentary on Ezekiel, Jerome suggests that the grammar may support the translation of Rosh as a proper noun. Obviously, he had some reservations about his translation. Clyde E. Billington Jr. "The Rosh People in History and Prophecy (Part One)," *Michigan Theological Journal* 3, no. 1 (Spring 1992): 57–61.

6. C. F. Keil, *Ezekiel, Daniel, Commentary on the Old Testament,* trans. James Martin (Grand Rapids, MI: Eerdmans, 1982), 159; Wilhelm Gesenius, *Gesenius' Hebrew-Chaldee Lexicon to the Old Testament* (Grand Rapids, MI: Eerdmans, 1949), 752.

7. The ancient Greek translations of Symmachus and Theodotian also translated Rosh in Ezekiel 38–39 as a proper noun. Billington, "The Rosh People in History and Prophecy (Part One)," 59.

8. Clyde E. Billington Jr., "The Rosh People in History and Prophecy (Part Two)," *Michigan Theological Journal* 3, no. 1 (Spring 1992): 54–61.

9. G. A. Cooke, *A Critical and Exegetical Commentary on the Book of Ezekiel*, The International Critical Commentary, ed. (Edinburgh: T & T Clark, 1936), 408–9. John B. Taylor agrees. He says, "If a place-name *Rosh* could be vouched for, RV's *prince of Rosh, Meshech, and Tubal* would be the best translation." John B. Taylor, *Ezekiel: An Introduction & Commentary*, Tyndale Old Testament Commentaries, gen. ed. D. J. Wiseman (Downers Grove, IL: InterVarsity Press, 1969), 244. As is demonstrated in this chapter of our book, there was a well-known place in Ezekiel's day known as Rosh. Therefore, this is the superior translation. For an extensive, thorough presentation of the grammatical and philological support for taking Rosh as a place-name, see James D. Price, "Rosh: An Ancient Land Known to Ezekiel," *Grace Theological Journal* 6, no. 1 (1985): 67–89.

10. DeMar, *End Times Fiction*, 5.

11. Gesenius, *Gesenius' Hebrew-Chaldee Lexicon to the Old Testament*, 752.

12. In his original Latin version of the lexicon titled *Thesaurus Linguae Hebraeae et Chaldaeae Veteris Testamenti*, Gesenius has nearly one page of notes dealing with the word *Rosh* and the Rosh people mentioned in Ezekiel 38–39. This page of notes does not appear in any of the English translations of Gesenius' lexicon. Those who disagree with Gesenius have failed to refute his sizable body of convincing evidence identifying Rosh with Russia. Billington, "The Rosh People in History and Prophecy (Part One)," 62–3.

13. Billington, "The Rosh People in History and Prophecy (Part Two)," 145–6.

14. James D. Price, "Rosh: An Ancient Land Known to Ezekiel," 71–3. It is very likely that the name Rosh is actually derived from the name Tiras in Genesis 10:2 in the Table of Nations. Billington (Part Two, 166–7) notes the Akkadian tendency to drop or to change an intial *t* sound in a name especially if the initial *t* was followed by an *r* sound. If you drop the initial *T* from Tiras, you are left with *ras*. It makes sense for Ras or Rosh to be listed in Genesis 10 since all the other nations in Ezekiel 38:1–6 are also listed there.

15. Jon Ruthven, "Ezekiel's Rosh and Russia: A Connection?" *Bibliotheca Sacra* (October 1968): 332–3.

16. Clyde E. Billington Jr., "The Rosh People in History and Prophecy (Part Three)," *Michigan Theological Journal* 4, no. 1 (Spring 1993), 61. Edwin M. Yamauchi, a noted authority, is often quoted as the conclusive authority that Rosh cannot be Russia. He says that the name Rus, which the modern name Russia is based upon, did not come to the region until the Middle Ages, when it was brought by the Vikings. Edwin M. Yamauchi, *Foes from the Northern Frontier* (Grand Rapids, MI: Baker, 1982), 20.

    However, while Yamauchi is a respected scholar, his dogmatic conclusion stands in direct opposition to the substantial historical, geographical, and ethnological evidence presented by Gesenius, Price, Ruthven, and Billington.

17. C. Marvin Pate and J. Daniel Hays believe that Ezekiel 38–39 probably describe an end-time attack against God's people. However they go on to say that "the nations mentioned are probably symbolic representations of these enemies and not specific nations that will attack." If this is true, then why does Ezekiel take the time to specifically mention ten proper names? Why be so exact? Why not just say that "a vast group of nations will invade" if that's what you mean? As stated earlier, we believe that the contemporary counterparts to these ancient places will invade Israel in the end times.

CHAPTER FOUR

1. Personal letter from Gary North to Peter Lalonde, April 30, 1987, on file.

2. Don Matzat, "The Great Premillennial HOAX," *Issues, Etc.*, Internet edition, http://www.issuesetc.org/resource/journals/v1.htm (accessed November 13, 2003).

3. Gary DeMar, *End Times Fiction: A Biblical Consideration of the Left Behind Theology* (Nashville, TN: Thomas Nelson, 2001), 202–3.

4. Walter C. Kaiser Jr., *Toward an Old Testament Theology* (Grand Rapids, MI: Zondervan, 1978), 124–5.

5. Arnold Fruchtenbaum, *The Footsteps of the Messiah* (Tustin, CA: Ariel Ministries Press, 1983), 65.

6. Ibid., 67.

7. Ibid., 102–3.

8. Randall Price, *Jerusalem in Prophecy: God's Final Stage for the Final Drama* (Eugene, OR: Harvest House, 1998), 219.

9. Fruchtenbaum, *The Footsteps of the Messiah*, 68.

10. John F. Walvoord, *Prophecy in the New Millennium: A Fresh Look at Future Events* (Grand Rapids, MI: Kregel, 2001), 61–2.

11. Fruchtenbaum, *The Footsteps of the Messiah*, 311.

12. John F. Walvoord, *Israel in Prophecy* (Grand Rapids, MI: Zondervan, 1962), 26.

13. Price, *Jerusalem in Prophecy*, 220.

CHAPTER FIVE

1. Fundamental Baptists are one of the main groups who criticize the idea of left behind loved ones getting saved. David Cloud, "Left Behind: Tolerable Entertainment, Intolerable Theology," *Way of Life Literature* (2001) http://www.wayoflife.org/fbns/leftbehind.htm (accessed November 11, 2003). Cloud says that the Left Behind series challenges people to get saved NOW, before it's too late, but then turns around and leaves people with the impression that it's possible to wait and get saved later after the Rapture. Cloud rejects this idea based on 2 Thessalonians 2:8–11.

2. Tim LaHaye has written a book that emphasizes the aspect of Bible prophecy that often gets completely overlooked. Tim LaHaye, *The Merciful God of Prophecy* (Nashville: Warner Faith, 2002).

3. David Jeremiah, *Escape the Coming Night*, Study Guide, vol. 2 (Dallas, TX: Word Publishing, 1997), 66.

4. Arnold Fruchtenbaum, *The Footsteps of the Messiah: A Study of the Sequence of Prophetic Events* (San Antonio: Ariel Press, 1982), 176.

CHAPTER SIX

1. Those who deny a future seven-year time of tribulation insist that there is no gap between the end of the sixty-ninth week in A.D. 33 and the beginning of the seventieth week. They see them as running consecutively. Gary DeMar, *End Times Fiction: A Biblical Consideration of the Left Behind Theology* (Nashville, TN: Thomas Nelson, 2001), 42–52. However, there are at least two insurmountable problems with this view. First, the text of Daniel 9:26–27 clearly denotes a gap of at least thirty-seven years between the end of the sixty-ninth and the beginning of the seventieth week (the time between the triumphal entry in A.D. 33 and the destruction of Jerusalem in A.D. 70). Second, if you don't put a gap of years between the sixty-ninth and seventieth weeks, you have the seventy weeks ending in about A.D. 40. And what great event happened that year? Nothing! De Mar (*End Times Fiction*, 50–1) tries to fit the destruction of Jerusalem in A.D. 70 into the seventieth week, but to do that, the final seven years has to be extended to at least thirty-seven years. This kind of twisting to make the numbers fit is contrary to sound biblical interpretation.

James Montgomery Boice, a well-known Bible expositor, faces this issue head-on and recognizes the necessity of a gap of time before the final seven years unfold.

> But what about the last week? What of the final seven years of the 490-year series? This is a puzzle for almost everyone due to the fact that if we simply add seven years to what we have already calculated, we come to the year A.D. 38 (or 46), and nothing of any particular importance happened in that year.... But I tend to think those people are right who see a break in the fulfillment of prophecy at this point. According to them, the fulfillment of this uniquely Jewish prophecy is suspended while the gospel is preached to the Gentiles and the full number of the church is brought in, a church encompassing people from all walks of life, all races and all nations. Then after the members of the church are fully gathered the prophecy will begin to unfold once more with a final week of acute suffering and persecution for the Jewish nation. In this view the last week of Daniel would coincide with a seven-year period of great tribulation mentioned elsewhere. I think there is support for this in Jesus' reference to "the abomination that causes desolation" mentioned in this passage (v. 27) as well as in Daniel 11:31 and 12:11 as something not to happen immediately, but to be experienced at the very end of the age (Matt. 24:15).

James Montgomery Boice, *Daniel: An Expositional Commentary* (Grand Rapids, MI: Zondervan, 1989), 109–10. For a thorough discussion of the seventy weeks prophecy of Daniel, see Thomas Ice, "The Seventy Weeks of Daniel," in *The End Times Controversy: The Second Coming Under Attack* (Eugene, OR: Harvest House, 2003), 307–53.

2. Those who disagree with the Left Behind view of the end times believe that the one who makes the covenant in Daniel 9:27 is not Antichrist, but Christ. They believe that the breaking of the covenant and making an end to sacrifices and offerings refers to Christ's death on the cross in A.D. 33. However, there are two stubborn problems with this view. First, the nearest antecedent to the pronoun "he" in Daniel 9:27 is the "prince who is to come," who is of the same people who destroyed the temple in A.D. 70. Clearly, this is a reference to the Romans. This cannot refer to Jesus since He was not Roman. This is a clear reference to the coming Antichrist who will arise from the reunited Roman Empire of the end times (see Daniel 7:8). Second, the Bible never indicates that Christ made a seven-year salvation covenant. He lived for about thirty-five years and ministered publicly for over three years. Nowhere do we find a particular seven-year period. Leon Wood sets forth seven convincing reasons for taking "he" in Daniel 9:27 as a reference to the coming prince or Antichrist. Leon Wood, *A Commentary on Daniel* (Grand Rapids, MI: Zondervan, 1973), 258.

3. John F. Walvoord, *Major Bible Prophecies: 37 Crucial Prophecies That Affect You Today* (Grand Rapids, MI: Zondervan, 1993), 319.

4. Irenaeus *Against Heresies*, 5.25.3–4.

5. Hippolytus, *Fragments from Commentaries, Daniel*, paragraph 22.

CHAPTER SEVEN

1. J. A. Seiss, *The Apocalypse: Lectures on the Book of Revelation* (Grand Rapids, MI: Zondervan, 1964), 397.

2. Benjamin Wills Newton, *Babylon: Its Future History and Doom*, 3d ed. (London: Houlston & Sons, 1890).

3. G. H. Pember, *Mystery Babylon the Great and the Mysteries of Catholicism: An Exposition of Revelation*, ed. G. H. Lang (Miami Springs, FL: Schoettle Co., 1988), 237–8.
4. Clarence Larkin, *The Book of Revelation* (Glenside, PA: Rev. Clarence Larkin Estate, 1919), 150.
5. Arthur W. Pink, *The Antichrist* (Grand Rapids, MI: Kregel, 1988), 237–8.
6. F. E. Marsh, "Will Babylon Be Rebuilt?," *Associates for Scriptural Knowledge*, September 30, 2002. http://askelm.com/prophecy/p021002.htm (accessed January 14, 2003).
7. William R. Newell, *The Book of Revelation* (Chicago: Moody Press, 1981), 268, 272.
8. One question that people often ask is, "How long would it take to build a city of this magnitude in modern Iraq?" It's one thing to say that a city will be built, but is it really feasible?

   Some might even suggest that if the rebuilding of Babylon is part of end-time events, then that means Jesus can't come back for at least twenty years. Obviously, it would take *years* to build a city like this. Or would it?

   Amazingly, we have a very recent example of a new city in the Middle East rising from the sand dunes. It's called Dubai Internet City. This new city is referred to as an oasis in the desert. Dubai Internet City is being heralded as the most ambitious engineering, business, and political project in the Middle East. The new city, located in the United Arab Emirates, is just a few kilometers from the city of Dubai. In 2001, Dubai Internet City had ten buildings with three hundred companies and thirty-five hundred users. The site contains lakes, landscapes, trees, and oases and occupies over four hundred acres. Currently, more than 350 additional applications from major enterprises for office space are being considered. During 2002, the city was slated to add fourteen more office buildings and 120 luxury residential villas. Here is the astounding part: *Dubai Internet City was designed, built, and launched in only twelve months.* While no one is claiming supercity status for this phenomenon in the dunes, its rise as an economic and technological center in such a brief time shows how quickly a city can rise in the Middle East desert. With incredible oil wealth and the power of Antichrist, Babylon could be rebuilt in a relatively short time.
9. Old Testament references to the day of the Lord: Isaiah 2:12; 13:6, 9; Ezekiel 13:5; 30:3; Joel 1:15; 2:1, 11, 31; 3:14; Amos 5:18, 20; Obadiah 15; Zephaniah 1:7, 14; Zechariah 14:1; Malachi 4:5. New Testament references: Acts 2:20; 1 Thessalonians 5:2; 2 Thessalonians 2:2; 2 Peter 3:10.
10. Jesus also uses the birth pains imagery from Isaiah 13:8 in Matthew 24:8.
11. Some have suggested that Isaiah 13–14 predicts the destruction of Babylon by the Assyrian King Sennacherib that occurred in December 689 B.C. It is true that Babylon was destroyed at that time. But we believe there are four serious problems with correlating Isaiah 13–14 with this destruction. First, there is no evidence of cosmic disturbances in 689 B.C. like those described in Isaiah 13:10. Second, the judgment on Babylon in 689 was not a worldwide judgment as depicted in Isaiah 13:11–12. Third, Babylon's destruction is simultaneous with Israel and Judah's restoration in Isaiah 14. This did not happen in 689 B.C. Fourth, the same language for Babylon's total destruction is used in Jeremiah 50:39–40 as is found in Isaiah 13. But we must remember that Jeremiah wrote in about 600 B.C., long after the destruction in 689. It appears that both Jeremiah and Isaiah are describing the same destruction of Babylon, not in 689 B.C. but in the end times, when Babylon is destroyed once and for all, never to be inhabited again. One might ask the question, "Does Isaiah have anything to say about the destruction of Babylon that occurred not long after he wrote?" I believe the answer is yes. It's interesting that Babylon's destruction is recorded by Isaiah again in 21:1–10. Why would he give another portrayal of Babylon's judgment after already spending two chapters on it earlier (13–14)? I believe that Isaiah 13–14 describes the final, eschatological, end-time destruction of Babylon. However, it seems that Isaiah 21:1–10

describes the near destruction of Babylon in December 689 B.C., at the hands of the Assyrians.

12. John F. Walvoord, *The Nations in Prophecy* (Grand Rapids: Zondervan, 1967), 63–4.
13. Larkin, *The Book of Revelation*, 58.
14. Gary DeMar holds the view that Babylon in Revelation 17–18 is the ancient city of Jerusalem and that these chapters describe its destruction in A.D. 70. *End Times Fiction: A Biblical Consideration of the Left Behind Theology* (Nashville, TN: Thomas Nelson Publishers, 2001), 124–9. While there are several problems with this view, four specific ones are fatal. First, Jerusalem and Babylon are distinguished from each other in Revelation 16:19, even as Babylon is introduced. The "great city," which is Jerusalem in the context, is distinguished from Babylon the Great. Second, Jerusalem does not sit on many waters (Revelation 17:15). Third, Jerusalem did not reign over the kings of the earth in A.D. 70 as Revelation 17:18 requires. Jerusalem did not even reign over *herself* in the first century; she was in political bondage to Rome. Fourth, in the first century, Jerusalem was never the world economic city described in Revelation 17–18. Even in one's wildest imagination, first-century Jerusalem did not even come close to the description of Babylon as the economic hub of the world.
15. Henry Morris, *The Revelation Record* (Wheaton, IL: Tyndale House, 1983), 323.
16. Ibid., 329.
17. Ibid., 348–9.
18. Charles H. Dyer, "The Identity of Babylon in Revelation 17–18," *Bibliotheca Sacra* 144 (October/December 1987): 441–3.

CHAPTER EIGHT

1. Gary DeMar, *End Times Fiction: A Biblical Consideration of the Left Behind Theology* (Nashville, TN: Thomas Nelson, 2001), 136.
2. DeMar (151) basically links LaHaye to these speculators when he says, "Further, we have to ask why LaHaye's understanding of Antichrist is so certain when hundreds of speculative prophecy writers throughout the centuries were equally certain of their choice."
3. Ibid., 137.
4. Ibid.
5. Ibid., 140.
6. The verb "is coming" in 1 John 2:18 is a futuristic present that "assumes the future coming of the antichrist to be as certain as the present reality." D. Edmond Hiebert, *The Epistles of John* (Greenville, SC: Bob Jones University Press, 1991), 109.
7. Here is a small sample of the scholars who believe 1 John speaks of a future personal Antichrist: F. F. Bruce, *The Epistles of John* (Grand Rapids, MI: Eerdmans Publishing Co., 1992), 64–8; Martyn Lloyd-Jones, *Walking with God: Life in Christ Volume 2, Studies in 1 John* (Wheaton, IL: Crossway Books, 1993), 98–101; R. C. H. Lenski, *The Interpretation of the Epistles of St. Peter, St. John and St. Jude* (Minneapolis, MN: Augsburg Publishing House, 1966), 430–2; James Montgomery Boice, *The Epistles of John* (Grand Rapids, MI: Zondervan Publishing House, 1979), 84–6; Simon J. Kistemaker, *James and I–III John*, New Testament Commentary (Grand Rapids, MI: Baker Book House, 1986), 275–6; I. Howard Marshall, *Epistles of John*, The New International Commentary on the New Testament, gen. ed. F. F. Bruce (Grand Rapids, MI: Eerdmans, 1978), 148–51; John R. W. Stott, *The Letters of John*, rev. ed., Tyndale New Testament Commentaries (Grand Rapids, MI: Eerdmans, 1994), 108–10; D. Edmond Hiebert, *The Epistles of John*, (Greenville, SC: Bob Jones University Press, 1991), 106–9. The only respected evangelical scholar I could find who did not hold that 1 John 2:18 refers to the coming of a future personal Antichrist was Brooke Foss Westcott, the great nineteenth-century scholar. And Westcott was not deci-

sive. All he said was that the passage is "not decisive as to St. John's teaching in regard to the coming of one great Antichrist, of which the others were preparatory embodiments." B. F. Westcott, *The Epistles of John* (Grand Rapids, MI: Eerdmans, 1966), 70. Bernard McGinn, who is not an evangelical Christian, but wrote a masterpiece on the subject of Antichrist, says that the use of the singular for antichrist in 1 John, "made it possible for most later Christians to believe in many antichrists as well as in the single final opposer predicted in 2 Thessalonians and the Apocalypse. Bernard McGinn, *Antichrist: Two Thousand Years of the Human Fascination with Evil* (San Francisco: Harper, 1994), 56.

8. Boice, *The Epistles of John*, 86.
9. Bruce, *The Epistles of John*, 65.
10. Ibid., 66–7.
11. Grant R. Jeffrey, *Prince of Darkness* (Toronto: Frontier Research, 1994), 29.
12. Ibid., 30.
13. J. Dwight Pentecost, *Will Man Survive?* (Grand Rapids, MI: Zondervan, 1971), 93.
14. Arthur W. Pink, *The Antichrist* (Grand Rapids, MI: Kregel Publications, 1988), 9.
15. DeMar says that LaHaye amalgamates divergent entities to "build an Antichrist." What DeMar ignores is that most scholars, even those who would disagree with LaHaye's overall end time view, agree that the same passages LaHaye uses all refer to the Antichrist. For instance, Martyn Lloyd-Jones says:

> It is very clear that other writers in different places are concerned about exactly the same thing. Second Thessalonians 2, again, is clearly a description of the same person, the same power, and the same condition. Then in Daniel 7–11 you will find clear descriptions of the same thing, and of course there is another classic passage in Revelation where you get an account of the two beasts, the one arising out of the sea and other arising out of the earth. All these are clearly references to the same power.

Lloyd-Jones, *Walking with God*, 98. Left Behind hasn't manufactured an Antichrist. The authors have simply brought all the relevant texts about him together in a compelling story format.
16. DeMar, *End Times Fiction*, 134–7.
17. *Didache* 16.4. DeMar maintains that the false messiahs in Mark 13:22 were present in the days before the destruction of the temple in A.D. 70 and that Nero was the Beast of Revelation 13. But the *Didache*, which was written after A.D. 70 refers to a future individual who will fulfill these prophecies.
18. Irenaeus, *Against Heresies*, 5.28.2
19. Ibid., 5.30.2.
20. Ibid., 5.25.3–4.
21. Hippolytus, *Antichrist*, 6. Cf. McGinn, *Antichrist: Two Thousand Years of the Human Fascination with Evil*, 61.
22. McGinn, 61.
23. Ibid., 63.
24. Cyril, *Catechetical Lectures* 15.12–15.
25. Jerome, *Commentary on Daniel 7:8; 11:39; 11:45*. Unlike most of the other early writers, Jerome did not support the view that the Antichrist would rebuild the temple in Jerusalem. He also strongly rejected any idea of a literal thousand-year reign of Christ. But he did believe in a future, personal Antichrist. Jerome believed that Daniel 7–11, 2 Thessalonians 2; Matthew 24; Revelation 17, and John 5:43 all related to the future Antichrist. John

Chrysostom also rejected the idea of a rebuilt temple, but he too believed in a personal Antichrist in the end times. *Homily 3 on 2 Thessalonians.*

26. McGinn, *Antichrist: Two Thousand Years of the Human Fascination with Evil,* 63.

CHAPTER NINE

1. Robert L. Thomas, *Revelation 8–22: An Exegetical Commentary* (Chicago: Moody Press, 1995), 179–80.

2. Ibid., 181.

3. Gary DeMar argues that the mark of the beast is symbolic, not a literal, visible mark. He says that the mark of the beast is the same as the mark given by God to the 144,000 in Revelation 7:3 and 14:1. We agree that the "sealing" in the foreheads of the 144,000 is probably symbolic and nonvisible. But one must keep in mind that different words are used in the original language of the text. In Revelation 7:3, the 144,000 are "sealed on their foreheads." And Revelation 14:1 says, "having His name and the name of His Father written on their foreheads." Whereas, with the Antichrist, the word *mark* (*charagma*) is used. The word *sealed* (*sphragizo*) is often used symbolically in the New Testament (John 3:33; 6:27; Romans 15:28; 2 Corinthians 1:22; Ephesians 1:13; 4:30). Walter Bauer, *A Greek-English Lexicon of the New Testament,* 2d ed. (Chicago: University of Chicago Press, 1957), 796. The word *mark,* on the other hand, refers to a literal, visible mark (cf. Acts 17:29). It means a "mark or stamp engraved, etched, branded, cut, imprinted" (Bauer, 876). It is always visible. The Holy Spirit uses different words for the seal of God and the mark of the beast. The one is often used symbolically, while the other is not. The one is often invisible, while the other is not.

4. Thomas, *Revelation 8–22,* 181. Other New Testament scholars agree that the mark of the beast will be visible. Robert H. Mounce, *The Book of Revelation,* The New International Commentary on the New Testament, gen. ed. F. F. Bruce (Grand Rapids, MI: Eerdmans, 1977), 262; G. R. Beasley-Murray, *The Book of Revelation,* The New Century Bible Commentary, gen. ed. Matthew Black (Grand Rapids, MI: Eerdmans, 1983), 218–9.

5. Sir William Ramsay, *The Letters to the Seven Churches* (New York: A.C. Armstrong, 1904), 107.

6. Thomas, *Revelation 8–22,* 182.

7. Ibid., 185. Gary DeMar, along with Kenneth Gentry, believes that the beast out of the sea in Revelation 13 was Nero. DeMar, *End Times Fiction: A Biblical Consideration of the Left Behind Theology* (Nashville, TN: Thomas Nelson, 2001), 142–5; Kenneth Gentry, *The Beast of Revelation* (Tyler, TX: Institute for Christian Economics, 1989). These writers point out that the name Neron Ceasar equals 666 and that the persecution under Nero lasted about forty-two months, or 1,260 days, as mentioned in Revelation 13:5. However, there are serious difficulties with identifying Nero with the beast out of the sea in Revelation 13. First, the book of Revelation was written in A.D. 95, after the reign of Nero was already over. Therefore, it can't be a prophecy about him. For a thorough discussion of the date of Revelation, see Mark Hitchcock, "The Stake in the Heart: The A.D. 95 Date of Revelation," in *The End Times Controversy* (Eugene, OR: Harvest House, 2003), 123–50. Second, DeMar and Gentry take the forty-two months of the beast's worldwide reign literally and then turn around and take almost every other number in Revelation symbolically. Why take the forty-two months literally and the others symbolically? There has to be some justification in the text for this inconsistent interpretation. Third, Nero never fulfilled the numerous clear statements in Revelation 13. Here are just a few examples: 1) the beast will be worshiped by the *entire* world, and "all who dwell on the earth will worship him, everyone whose name has not been written from the foundation of the world in the book of life of

the Lamb who has been slain" (Revelation 13:8); 2) he will force people to take his mark on their right hand or forehead to engage in any commercial transactions; 3) an image of him will be built that all the world must worship; 4) he will be slain and come back to life; and 5) he will have an associate, the false prophet, who will call down fire from heaven and give breath to the image. Clearly, none of these things was fulfilled during Nero's reign. Neither Nero nor any other Roman emperor ever marked the whole world with 666. But all of these prophecies will be fulfilled precisely in the coming Antichrist of the end times in a manner consistent with the end time view of Left Behind. Fourth, in order for Nero's name to equal 666, you have to use the precise title Neron Ceasar. No other form of his name will work. Moreover, if the relationship of 666 to Nero is so obvious, why did it take almost eighteen hundred years following Nero's death for anyone to make this connection between his name and 666? For a complete refutation of the view that Nero is the beast of Revelation 13, see Andy Woods, "Revelation 13 and the First Beast," in *The End Times Controversy* (Eugene, OR: Harvest House, 2003), 237–50.

CHAPTER   TEN

1. John F. Walvoord, *Oil, Armageddon and the Middle East Crisis* (Grand Rapids, MI: Zondervan, 1990), 227–8.
2. Ibid.

CHAPTER   ELEVEN

1. David L. Cooper, *The World's Greatest Library: Graphically Illustrated* (Los Angeles: Biblical Research Society, 1970), 11.
2. Gary DeMar, *End Times Fiction: A Biblical Consideration of the Left Behind Theology* (Nashville, TN: Thomas Nelson, 2001), 188.
3. Carl E. Olson, *Will Catholics Be "Left Behind"? A Catholic Critique of the Rapture and Today's Prophecy Preachers* (San Francisco: Ignatius Press, 2003), 242.
4. Tim LaHaye and Jerry B. Jenkins, *Are We Living in the End Times? Current Events Foretold in Scripture…and What They Mean* (Wheaton, IL: Tyndale House, 1999), 6.
5. *Webster's New Twentieth Century Dictionary*, Unabridged, 2nd ed., 1055.
6. *The Compact Edition of The Oxford English Dictionary* (New York: Oxford Press, 1971), s.v., "literal."
7. Paul Lee Tan, *The Interpretation of Prophecy* (Winona Lake, IN: Assurance, 1974), 29.
8. Bernard Ramm, *Protestant Biblical Interpretation: A Textbook of Hermeneutics*, 3rd ed. (Grand Rapids, MI: Baker Book House, 1970), 119.
9. This is essentially the interpretation given by John Calvin in his commentary. John Calvin, *Commentary on the Book of the Prophet Isaiah*, Vol. 1, translated from the original Latin by the Rev. William Pringle (Grand Rapids, MI: Baker Book House, 1979), 89–103.
10. *Tim LaHaye Prophecy Study Bible*, KJV (Chattanooga, TN: AMG, 2000), 691.
11. Charles C. Ryrie, *Dispensationalism* (Chicago: Moody Press, 1995), 80.
12. Roy B. Zuck, *Basic Bible Interpretation: A Practical Guide to Discovering Biblical Truth* (Wheaton, IL: Victor Books, 1991), 100.
13. Ibid., 100–1.
14. Tan, *The Interpretation of Prophecy*, 103.
15. Zuck, *Basic Bible Interpretation*, 77.
16. Ryrie, *Dispensationalism*, 80–1.
17. LaHaye, "How to Study Bible Prophecy," xiii.

18. Tim LaHaye, *Revelation Unveiled*, rev. ed. (Grand Rapids, MI: Zondervan, 1999), 323.
19. John F. Walvoord, *The Revelation of Jesus Christ* (Chicago: Moody Press, 1966), 277, quoted in LaHaye, *Revelation Unveiled*, 307.
20. LaHaye, "How to Study Bible Prophecy," xiii.
21. DeMar, *End Times Fiction*, 188–90.
22. Ramm, *Protestant Biblical Interpretation*, 126.
23. DeMar, *End Times Fiction*, 3. DeMar's citation of LaHaye is from Tim LaHaye, *No Fear of the Storm: Why Christians Will Escape All the Tribulation* (Sisters, OR: Multnomah, 1992), 240.
24. Tan, *The Interpretation of Prophecy*, 63.
25. Ryrie, *Dispensationalism*, 81.
26. John F. Walvoord, *Prophecy: 14 Essential Keys to Understanding the Final Drama* (Nashville, TN: Thomas Nelson, 1993), 11.
27. For a more comprehensive treatment defending literal interpretation, see Robert L. Thomas, *Evangelical Hermeneutics: The New Versus the Old* (Grand Rapids, MI: Kregel, 2002).

CHAPTER TWELVE
1. Carl E. Olson, *Will Catholics Be "Left Behind"? A Catholic Critique of the Rapture and Today's Prophecy Preachers* (San Francisco: Ignatius Press, 2003), 42–3.
2. Charles C. Ryrie, *What Is Dispensationalism?* (Pamphlet published by Dallas Theological Seminary, [1980], 1986), 1.
3. Charles C. Ryrie, *Dispensationalism* (Chicago: Moody Press, [1966], 1995).
4. Ibid., 25.
5. Ibid., 26.
6. Ibid., 26–7.
7. Ibid., 29.
8. Ibid.
9. Paul David Nevin, "Some Major Problems in Dispensational Interpretation" (Th. D. dissertation, Dallas Seminary, 1965), 97.
10. Renald E. Showers, *There Really Is a Difference! A Comparison of Covenant and Dispensational Theology* (Bellmawr, NJ: The Friends of Israel Gospel Ministry, 1990), 27, 30.
11. Ryrie, *Dispensationalism*, 40.
12. Earl D. Radmacher, "The Current Status of Dispensationalism and Its Eschatology," ed. Kenneth S. Kantzer and Stanley N. Gundry, *Perspectives on Evangelical Theology* (Grand Rapids, MI: Baker, 1979), 171.
13. Ryrie, *Dispensationalism*, 39.
14. Lewis Sperry Chafer, *Dispensationalism* (Dallas: Seminary Press, 1936), 107, as cited in Ryrie, *Dispensationalism*, 39.
15. Arnold G. Fruchtenbaum, "Israel and the Church" in *Issues in Dispensationalism* (Chicago: Moody Press, 1994), 126.
16. Showers, *There Really Is a Difference!* 53.
17. Ryrie, *Dispensationalism*, 213.
18. Showers, *There Really Is a Difference!* 49–52.
19. Ryrie, *What Is Dispensationalism?* 7.

CHAPTER THIRTEEN

1. Tim LaHaye and Jerry B. Jenkins, *Are We Living in the End Times? Current Events Foretold in Scripture…and What They Mean* (Wheaton, IL: Tyndale House, 1999), 112–3.

2. Gary DeMar, *End Times Fiction: A Biblical Consideration of the Left Behind Theology* (Nashville, TN: Thomas Nelson, 2001), 19.

3. Charles C. Ryrie, *Dispensationalism* (Chicago: Moody Press, 1995), 15–6.

4. John F. Walvoord, *The Blessed Hope and the Tribulation* (Grand Rapids, MI: Zondervan, 1976), 24–5.

5. Kurt Aland, *A History of Christianity*, vol. 1 (Philadelphia: Fortress Press, 1985), 87–93. Millard J. Erickson, *Contemporary Options in Eschatology* (Grand Rapids, MI: Baker Book House, 1977), 112. J. Barton Payne, *The Imminent Appearing of Christ* (Grand Rapids, MI: Eerdmans, 1962), 12–9.

6. Larry V. Crutchfield, "The Blessed Hope and the Tribulation in the Apostolic Fathers" in Thomas Ice and Timothy Demy, eds., *When the Trumpet Sounds* (Eugene, OR: Harvest House, 1995), 103.

7. Ibid., 88–101.

8. *The Shepherd of Hermas* 1.4.2.

9. For more information on this matter, see Timothy J. Demy and Thomas D. Ice, "The Rapture and an Early Medieval Citation," *Bibliotheca Sacra* 152, no. 607 (July–Sept 1995): 306–17.

10. DeMar, *End Times Fiction*, 219.

11. Dorothy deF. Abrahamse, introduction to *The Byzantine Apocalyptic Tradition*, by Paul J. Alexander (Berkeley: University of California Press, 1985), 1–2.

12. Francis X. Gumerlock, *The Day and the Hour: A Chronicle of Christianity's Perennial Fascination with Predicting the End of the World* (Powder Springs, GA: American Vision, 2000).

13. Ibid., 80.

14. Francis X. Gumerlock, "A Rapture Citation in the Fourteenth Century," *Bibliotheca Sacra* 159, no. 635 (July–Sept 2002): 362.

15. Gumerlock's translation of the Latin text in ibid., 354–5.

16. Ibid., 361.

17. Paul Boyer, *When Time Shall Be No More: Prophecy Belief in Modern American Culture* (Cambridge, MA: Belknap Press, 1992), 75.

18. Paul N. Benware, *Understanding End Times Prophecy: A Comprehensive Approach* (Chicago: Moody Press, 1995), 197–8.

19. Frank Marotta, *Morgan Edwards: An Eighteenth Century Pretribulationist* (Morganville, NJ: Present Truth, 1995), 10–2.

20. The entire title of Asgill's work is as follows: *An argument proving, that according to the covenant of Eternal Life revealed in the Scriptures, Man may be translated from hence into that Eternal Life, without passing through Death, although the Human Nature of Christ himself could not be thus translated till he had passed through Death.*

21. William Bramley-Moore, *The Church's Forgotten Hope or, Scriptural Studies on the Translation of the Saints* (Glasgow: Hobbs, 1905), 322.

22. Marotta, *Morgan Edwards*.

23. Morgan Edwards, *Two Academical Exercises on Subjects Bearing the following Titles; Millennium, Last-Novelties* (Philadelphia: Self-published, 1788). The spelling of all Edwards's quotes has been modernized.

24. Roy A. Huebner, *Precious Truths Revived and Defended Through J. N. Darby*, vol. 1 (Morganville, NJ: Present Truth, 1991), 63–77.

25. Dave MacPherson, *The Unbelievable Pre-Trib Origin* (Kansas City: Heart of America Bible Society, 1973); *The Late Great Pre-Trib Rapture* (Kansas City: Heart of America Bible Society, 1974); *The Great Rapture Hoax* (Fletcher, NC: New Puritan Library, 1983); *Rapture?* (Fletcher, NC: New Puritan Library, 1987); *The Rapture Plot* (Simpsonville, SC: Millennium III, 1994).

26. The following books are some of those that have the full text of Macdonald's utterance: MacPherson's *Cover-Up* and *Hoax*; R. A. Huebner, *The Truth of the Pre-Tribulation Rapture Recovered* (Millington, NJ: Present Truth, 1976), 67–9; Hal Lindsey, *The Rapture: Truth or Consequences* (New York: Bantam, 1983), 169–72; William R. Kimball, *The Rapture: A Question of Timing* (Grand Rapids, MI: Baker Book House, 1985), 44–7.

27. Thomas D. Ice, "Why the Doctrine of the Pretribulational Rapture Did Not Begin with Margaret Macdonald," *Bibliotheca Sacra* 147 (1990), 158, 161.

28. Walvoord, *The Blessed Hope and the Tribulation*, 47.

29. R. A. Huebner, *Precious Truths Revived and Defended Through J. N. Darby*, vol. 1 (Morganville, NJ: Present Truth, 1991).

30. Ibid., 17.

31. Ibid., 19.

32. Ibid., 18.

33. Ibid., 23.

34. Ibid., 24.

35. J. N. Darby, "Reflections upon the Prophetic Inquiry and the Views Advanced in it" *The Collected Writings of J. N. Darby*, vol. 2 (Winschoten, Netherlands: H. L. Heijkoop, reprint 1971), 1–31.

36. Ibid., 16–8, 25, 30.

37. Timothy P. Weber, *Living in the Shadow of the Second Coming: American Premillennialism 1875-1982* (Grand Rapids, MI: Zondervan, 1983), 21–2.

38. Richard R. Reiter, *The Rapture: Pre-, Mid-, or Post-Tribulational?* (Grand Rapids, MI: Zondervan, 1984), 236.

39. William E. Bell, *A Critical Evaluation of the Pretribulation Rapture Doctrine in Christian Eschatology* (Ph.D. Dis., New York University, 1967), 60–1, 64–5.

40. Huebner, *Precious Truths*, 13.

41. Ibid., 67.

42. See MacPherson, *Rapture Plot*.

43. Columba Graham Flegg, *'Gathered Under Apostles' A Study of the Catholic Apostolic Church* (Oxford: Clarendon Press, 1992), 436.

44. Grayson Carter, *Anglican Evangelicals: Protestant Secessions from the Via Media, c. 1800–1850* (Oxford: Oxford University Press, 2001), 226.

45. Edward Irving, "Signs of the Times in the Church," *The Morning Watch*, vol. 2 (1830), 156.

46. Walvoord, *The Blessed Hope and the Tribulation*, 47.

END TIMES ANSWERS

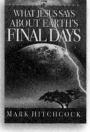

WHAT ON EARTH IS GOING ON?
Pierce through the post-9/11 clouds of sensationalism and skepticism with prophecy expert Mark Hitchcock as he gives a balanced view of today's major global developments signaling Christ's return.
ISBN 1-57673-853-1

IS AMERICA IN BIBLE PROPHECY?
Will America suffer a great fall? Find out what's in store for the world's superpower in the coming days with prophecy scholar and pastor Mark Hitchcock.
ISBN 1-57673-496-X

THE COMING ISLAMIC INVASION OF ISRAEL
Mark Hitchcock shows how events today may be setting the stage for the fulfillment of Ezekiel's prediction—a Russian-Islamic confederation of nations will finally invade Israel and be destroyed by God.
ISBN 1-59052-048-3

IS THE ANTICHRIST ALIVE TODAY?
Is the Antichrist alive today, right now, in this generation? Prophecy expert Mark Hitchcock discusses five current events preparing the world for the Antichrist's reign.
ISBN 1-59052-075-0

SEVEN SIGNS OF THE END TIMES
Are you noticing the symptoms of the end of the world? Get an expert opinion. Find out seven specific signs the Bible says to look for.
ISBN 1-59052-129-3

WHAT JESUS SAYS ABOUT EARTH'S FINAL DAYS
Jesus spent twice as much time telling His followers to prepare for His return than He did describing the actual event. What was His point? You need to be ready.
ISBN 1-59052-208-7

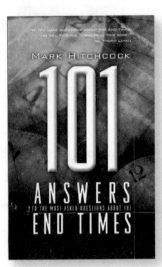

101 ANSWERS TO THE MOST ASKED QUESTIONS ABOUT THE END TIMES

The end is near! *Or is it?* The Antichrist is alive and well today! *Or is he?* The church is about to be raptured and will certainly escape the Tribulation...*right?* When it comes to the end times, there's so much confusion. *Would somebody please shoot straight with me?* Finally, someone has. Gifted scholar and pastor Mark Hitchcock walks you gently through Bible prophecy in an engaging, user-friendly style. Hitchcock's careful examination of the topic will leave you feeling informed and balanced in your understanding of events to come...in our time?

ISBN 1-57673-952-X

THE SECOND COMING OF BABYLON

Stirrings in Iraq—Is Babylon Back? The Bible says that Babylon will be rebuilt and become the economic center of the world. Even now the ruins of the ancient city—just sixty miles south of Baghdad, Iraq—are quietly stirring. What does it mean for America? For Israel? For every person alive today? Are we living in the last days of earth as we know it? Find out, from Bible prophecy expert Mark Hitchcock.

ISBN 1-59052-251-6

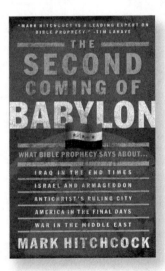

For More information on

Left Behind Products

visit
www.leftbehind.com